The Ultimate Website Builder SEO Handbook

Roggie Clark

Master HTML, CSS, and JavaScript With This One Book

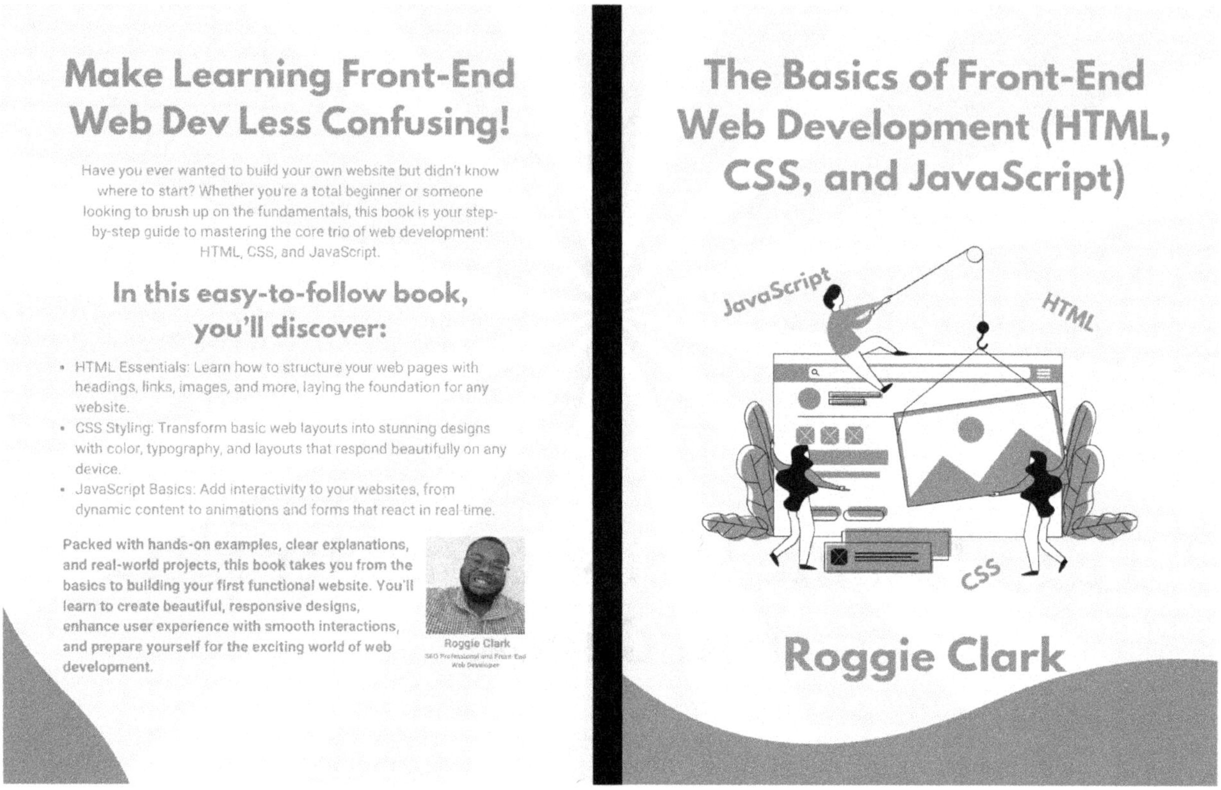

To learn all three coding languages, check out the full book.

https://www.amazon.com/Basics-Front-End-Development-HTML-JavaScript-ebook/dp/B0DJ147B15

Master HTML, CSS, and Javascript With These Books

The Basics of JavaScript Coding For Beginners: Learn Basic JavaScript Programming Concepts in less than 50 pages

https://www.amazon.com/Basics-JavaScript-Coding-Beginners-Programming-ebook

The Basics of HTML (Hypertext Markup Language) Coding For Beginners : Learn Foundational HTML Programming Concepts

https://www.amazon.com/Basics-Hypertext-Markup-Language-Beginners-ebook

The Basics of CSS (Cascading Style Sheets) Coding For Beginners: Learn Basic CSS Programming Concepts

https://www.amazon.com/Basics-Cascading-Sheets-Coding-Beginners-ebook

Master SEO With This One Book

https://www.amazon.com/ABCs-Search-Engine-Optimization-Page-ebook

Checkout These Books to Learn More SEO From Me

Creating An SEO Strategy 101: Learn How to Create An Effective SEO Content, Website and Link-Building Strategy From Scratch

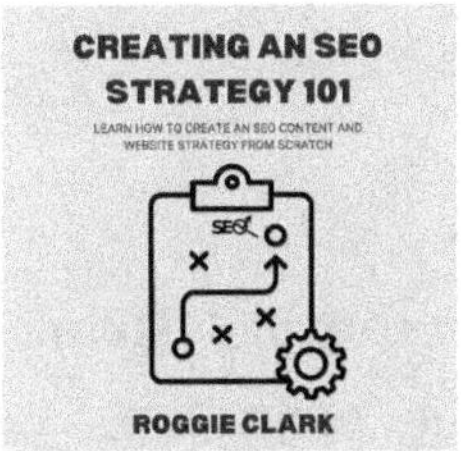

https://www.amazon.com/Creating-SEO-Strategy-101-Link-Building-ebook

Technical SEO Handbook: Learn How to Audit and Fix Advanced Technical SEO Issues

https://www.amazon.com/Technical-SEO-Handbook-Learn-Issues-ebook

The SEO and Web Developer Collaboration Guide

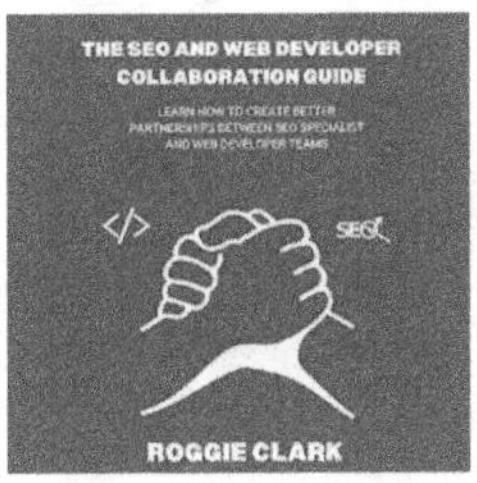

https://www.amazon.com/SEO-Web-Developer-Collaboration-Guide-ebook

Copyright

Title: The Ultimate Website Builder SEO Handbook
Author: Roggie Clark

Published by Kindle Direct Publishing
410 Terry Ave N
Seattle, Washington, 98109
United States
https://kdp.amazon.com/en_US

Cover Design: Roggie Clark
Editing: Renee' Clark

ISBN: 979-8-218-19232-7

Printed in the United States of America

Disclaimer

The views and opinions expressed in this book are those of the author and do not necessarily reflect the official policy or position of any individual, company, or organization cited or referenced in the text. The author is not affiliated with any of the individuals, companies, or organizations mentioned in the text, nor does the author receive any form of compensation for citing or referencing them. Some sample scenarios in this text are fictitious. Any similarity to actual persons, living or dead, is coincidental.

The professional information (strategies, tips, and concepts) in this text is distributed on an "as is" basis, without warranty. While every precaution has been taken in the preparation of the text to ensure all information is accurate, neither the author nor the publisher shall have any liability to any person or entity with respect to any loss or damage caused or alleged to be caused directly or indirectly by the instructions contained in this text or by the computer software and hardware products described in it.

The author nor the publisher guarantees any specific results or outcomes, and the information provided in this text should not be construed as professional advice. Readers should always consult with a qualified professional before making any significant changes to their website or business.

By reading this text, you agree that the author nor the publisher is responsible for any direct, indirect, incidental, or consequential damages that may arise from the use of the information provided. You assume full responsibility for any actions taken based on the information presented in this text.

Table of Contents

Section 1: Introduction and Essentials

Chapter 1: Introduction

When it comes to building a great website, you have a lot of options. A domain name, which content management system to use, what colors and fonts to use. You might even decide to build a website from scratch, or even have a designer help you. One thing for certain is there is no shortage of things to think about when it comes to building a website.

The goal of this book is to help you demystify the whole website-building process and instead focus on what really matters, and that is getting traffic to your site! Another thing for certain is that you are going to see ad after ad hyping you up on the newest and greatest website-building software, but you will rarely, if ever, see ads on how to actually get people to your site.

If you are building a website, chances are you are not just doing it to show off. You are doing it to make money and hopefully grow a successful business around it. So, without a doubt, I can tell you that this book is going to help you avoid all the hype and get right to the good stuff!

Let me tell you how this book is going to help you. First I start really simple by just talking about the basic things you need to start a website like web hosting, a domain, etc. This is in **Chapter 1**, and **2**. Then in **Chapters 3**, **4**, **5**, **6** and **7** - I talk about how to actually start building your website, to do this you need to have an understanding of the "coding languages" HTML, CSS, and JavaScript. You need to know them in order to create a website from scratch. Also I talk about how you can streamline the creation process by getting an out-of-box website solution called a CMS. This may be easier for non web developers to use.

Once we get done with that, we are going to talk about how to actually get traffic to your website, this is in **Chapters 8**, and **9**. You definitely don't want to miss these chapters because this all about making sure your website is not just sitting there, but actually becoming a money making opportunity. I do this by teaching you SEO (Search Engine Optimization). Then I'll wrap everything up in **Chapter 10**, with some more additional tips for having long-term success with your website.

This book is robust, and the perfect handbook for beginner, novice, and advanced website creators. By the time you are done with this book you will be on the road to having a website that gets the job done. With that being said, let's get started with Chapter 2.

Chapter 2: Website Basics

Okay, so I think it is best to start slow, and that is to start with just the basics. Before you start building a website, I think it is important to first make sure you have a solid foundation to build with.

You can start yourself out right by first picking out a domain name, thinking about where you want users to go, also known as the URL structure of your website. Also thinking about your Sitemap and how you want search engines to crawl your website. All these things fall under the category of just basic website hygiene, but you'd be surprised how many people forget to address these things first.

There are too many website owners who rush to create the best-looking website on the planet but spend absolutely zero time even thinking about how an actual user is going to make use of it. I am going to help you with getting the basics correct. Let's go over each piece.

Web Hosting

For a website to be accessible on the Internet and thus accessible to search engines, the website must be "housed" or stored on a **Server**. A server can also be thought of as a digital neighborhood.

Many web admins may choose to *house* their websites on their own servers. However, generally, hosting is outsourced to a "web hosting service" or companies that have a network/ collection of servers that they then "rent" out for other people to house their website.

Although this may seem like a good idea, using shared hosting can lead to slow website performance and delayed usability.

This can happen due to a variety of factors, such as competition with other websites for server space, the size of the server, how fast the server can process requests, the amount of data that can be transferred at one time, and the amount of traffic the website receives.

In my experience, the only way to mitigate hosting issues is often to upgrade (pay for) a better package or to have a dedicated server, which requires an investment. Both methods are typically expensive for a small business; therefore, drastically improving performance is not always feasible.

Last Words about Web Hosting

Generally, you should choose web hosting that fits your needs. Now that we discussed web hosting, let us talk about the next most important thing: your website and webpage's location on the Internet better known as a **URL**.

URLs

A **Uniform Resource Locator (URL)**, also called a "web address," is the location of a website or file on the Internet.

Here's an example of a basic URL:

`https://www.domain.com/folder/web-page`

Before we dive into URL structure, I want to preface that URLs can be rather *tricky* to comprehend because they can include many components that can be abstract.

Nevertheless, don't worry; in the next section, you can refer to this simple diagram below to clearly understand what I mean.

With that note in mind, let's break down the structure of the URL:

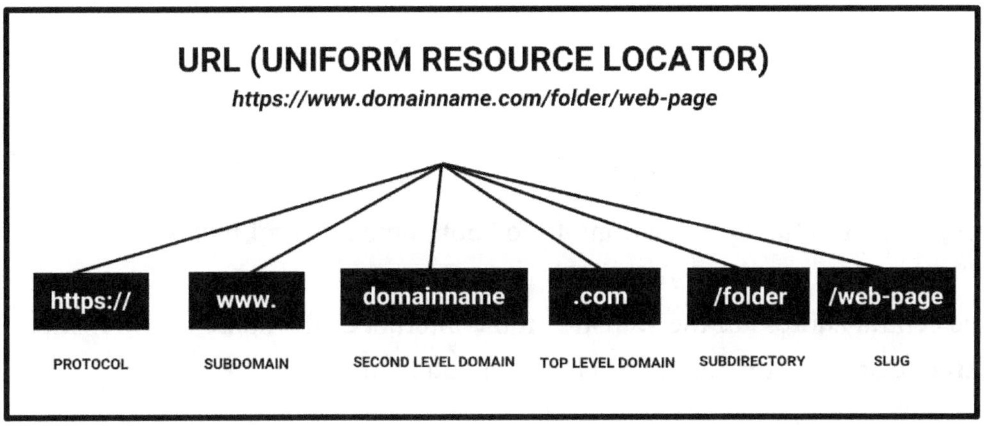

The first piece of a URL is: `https: //` this stands for the *Protocol* or the way the website is accessed.

In this case, it is the **HyperText Transfer Protocol Secure (HTTPS)** which is considered to be the most secure way of transferring information on the Internet, as opposed to `http: //` which is just **HyperText Transfer Protocol (HTTP)**, which is often avoided because of its less secure nature.

Next, `WWW` stands for the World Wide Web. This statement is used to be able to access other webpages in the online directory. `WWW` is also an example of a **Subdomain** - which can be thought of as a "subdivision" of a *domain* where additional webpages and content can be stored.

`domainname` is the name of the website. It can also be referred to as the **Second level domain (SLD)** or just simply the *domain.*

The `.com` indicates the type of **Top Level Domain (TLD)**, used in the **Domain Naming System (DNS)**. In this case, it is **commercial** `.com` but other common TLDs are `.edu` for education or `.org` for organizations.

`/folder` indicates the current **Subdirectory** or holding place of the webpage, and lastly, `/web-page/` is the name of the webpage, it can also be referred to as a **Slug**.

Last Words about URL Structure

URLs are the main access point a user has to a website and/or webpage. I am bringing up URLs because you need to make sure you "write" good ones. As in you properly name them to make finding content easier. In the next section, we will explore **Domains**, which heavily relate to URLs.

Domains

I discussed domains a bit in the URL section of the book, here's a brief recap:

- A **Domain** is the central address of the website on the internet or the name of a website, for **`bouncerank.com, bouncerank`** is the domain name
- **`WWW`** stands for the **Subdomain**, which in this case is the World Wide Web directory
- The **Top Level Domain (TLD**) (e.g., .com, .edu, .org, .net, .jobs)
- The **Second Level Domain** (**SLD**) , which is the name of the actual website, it's usually what people will remember and use to find a website.

For my old website, Bounce Rank, my website's domain is `https://` which as I mentioned in the last section, stands for Hypertext transfer protocol secure, next is `WWW` for world wide web, which is the **subdomain** we are accessing, then `bouncerank` which is my **SLD** (it is not case-sensitive), and last is `.com`, for my **TLD** which is the final very important piece.

Together here is the URL of my website:

`https://www.bouncerank.com`

Now right now you may be wondering, "how do I go about picking a domain name?"

When choosing domain names, generally you want to choose a name that is:

- Easy to read
- Easy to type/spell
- Contains no misspellings
- Contains a common TLD (.com,.net, .edu)
- Avoids spaces, hyphens, dots, double letters or any symbols
- Contains only letters

Last Words about Domains

A website's domain name is equivalent to the address of a home or building, it is used to identify a particular web property on the internet. It is also what users will type into their web browser to access the website.

So when choosing a domain name for a website, my best advice is to keep it simple, and easy to remember. But also do your research to see what domains are available and to ensure that you are not infringing on someone else's trademark, copyright, or intellectual property. When in doubt, using your business name is usually a good place to start.

Robots.txt File

The **Robots.txt file**, is a file generally stored on a website at the URL slug: `/robots.txt` It was invented as a way to tell search engine web crawlers which directories or web folders on the website the crawler can access. The file can also be used to specify which folders the crawlers are "blocked" from or *should not/cannot* access on a website.

In a nutshell, the robots.txt file contains "directives" "rules" and "references" - which can be thought of as a request to search crawlers regarding the directories you wish to be visited or ignored.

Here's an example of a basic file:

```
User-agent: *
Disallow: /author/
Allow: /author/archives/

Sitemap: https://bouncerank.com/sitemap_index.xml
```

Last Words about Robots.txt File

Despite the intricacies of the Robots.txt file, it is not necessarily *required* to be included on a website. However, it is generally best practice to include one.

The reason is, the file gives webmasters the opportunity to tell search engines what folders they should crawl. By being able to control what is indexed and crawled, search crawlers can better prioritize indexing content that matters to users, and avoid wasting crawl resources on content that is not relevant. This matters for SEO, and getting organic traffic to your site.

XML Sitemap

Another file stored on a website that tells search engine crawlers about the organization of a website's pages is known as the **XML Sitemap**. It is generally stored on a website at the URL slug: `/sitemap.xml`

The file is essentially a "map" that shows web crawlers how to access each *URL* or location of content on the domain; hence the name "sitemap".

Additionally, the file indicates to search crawlers the priority/ hierarchy of pages on the website; and lastly, it can be used to alert search engines about changes to the website.

Here is an example of a basic XML sitemap configuration:

```
<?xml version="1.0" encoding="UTF-8"?>
<urlset xmlns="http://www.sitemaps.org/schemas/sitemap/0.9">
<url>
        <loc>https://bouncerank.com/author/rajseo333/</loc>
    </url>
    <url>
        <loc>https://bouncerank.com/what-is-seo/</loc>
    </url>
    <url>
        <loc>https://bouncerank.com/how-to-write-seo-specialist-cover-letter/</loc>
    </url>
    </urlset>
```

Last Words about XML Sitemaps

Like Robots.txt files, XML Sitemaps are not required by search engines and do not speed up crawling and/or indexing. Nevertheless, it is good website hygiene to include one on a website because again it helps with getting organic users to your website.

Last Words

As I said earlier, it is important to think about these types of things first, especially the URL path structure, what web hosting you want to use, and the domain you wish to use. These things are the foundation. Your site will grow and change over time, but making sure that the basics are squared away first is key. Now, let's get into the actual building blocks that make up a website, and that is the "code" or the digital languages that are used to construct a website: HTML, CSS, and JavaScript.

Section 2: Creating Your Website

Chapter 3: HTML (Hypertext Markup Language)

HyperText Markup Language (HTML) is the *standard markup* or computer code that is used to create and structure content on the web. Web browsers can "render" (display) HTML on a user's computer screen, in a format readable for the user.

Here's an example of a basic HTML document:

```
<!DOCTYPE html>
<html>
     <head>
           </head>
          <body>

          </body>
</html>
```

Key Components of An HTML Document

Let's break down this example into its components, as you can see, HTML documents include several key elements such as: `<!DOCTYPE html>`. This is the statement that declares that the document is an HTML document. All HTML documents must include this statement.

Additionally, The `<!DOCTYPE html>` declaration is used to inform the browser which version of HTML the page is written in. In modern web development, we use **HTML5**, and `<!DOCTYPE html>`is the declaration for HTML5.

Next is the `<html>` element, which defines the start of the HTML document, it "wraps" around everything that's displayed on a webpage. It marks the beginning and end of the document.

Next is the `<head>` element. This tag represents the top or beginning of the HTML document. Additionally, it may contain meta-information about the page. This can include the title, meta tags (used for search engine optimization), and links to external resources such as JavaScript and/or CSS files. It does not contain content that will be visible to users.

Lastly, the `<body>` section contains the actual content that will be displayed on the webpage. It includes text, images, links, buttons, and anything else users will interact with.

There are additional, HTML tags that you will commonly see but before doing that I believe that it is important to establish a baseline understanding of HTML syntax first.

How to Write HTML Properly

When writing HTML it is important to know the proper way to do it, this ensures that your code is easy to read and follow. Here's what you should know about HTML syntax:

1. Closing Tags and Self-Closing Elements:

- Most elements have **opening** (`<head>`) and **closing** tags (`</head>`). The content goes between these tags. As you can see, the `/` is used to represent the closing tag.
- Some tags, like `<img>` or `<br>`, are **self-closing** and don't need a closing tag. (We explore what these tags represent in the *common HTML Tags* section)
- Always make sure to close your tags (for elements that require a closing tag) and use self-closing syntax for elements like `<img>` and `<br>`.

---

2. Not Case-Sensitive:

- HTML tags are **not case-sensitive**, but the convention is to write them in **lowercase** (e.g., `<body>`, not `<Body>` or `<BODY>`). This improves readability and consistency.

---

3. HTML Attributes:

- Attributes provide additional information about an element. They are always written in the **opening tag** and come in name/value pairs, like **`href="https://example.com"`** in an *anchor tag* (`<a>`). We will explore *anchor tags* in greater detail in the *common HTML Tags* section
- The attribute value should be enclosed in **double quotes** (`"  "`), though single quotes (`'  '`) are technically allowed.

Example:

```
<a href="https://example.com" target="_blank">Visit Example</a>
```

---

4. Nesting and Proper Tag Hierarchy:

- HTML elements can be **nested** inside one another. However, proper **tag hierarchy** is crucial.
- Always close tags in the **reverse order** in which they were opened.

As you can recall from the previous code snippet I showed above:

```
<!DOCTYPE html>
<html>
     <head>
          </head>
          <body>

          </body>
</html>
```

Inside of the `<!DOCTYPE html>` element, the `<html>` is nested inside of it, and then nested inside of it, is the `<head>` element, and nested inside the `<html>` element is the `<body>` element.

Here is an example of <u>incorrect </u>nesting:

```
<!DOCTYPE html>
<html>
     <head><body></body></head>
</html>
```

As you can see the `<body>` element is incorrectly nested in the `<head>` element.

---

5. Indentation and Readability:

- Use consistent **indentation** to organize nested elements. This improves the readability of the code, especially for larger documents.
- Typically, a **two or four-space** indentation is used for each level of nesting.

Again recalling the code snippet example from above, notice how each tag starts on a new "line" again this improves readability.

```
<!DOCTYPE html>
<html>
     <head>
           </head>
          <body>

          </body>
</html>
```

---

6. HTML Comments:

- Comments are helpful for leaving notes in the code for future reference. They do not affect how the webpage is displayed.
- Comments are added using the syntax: `<!-- Comment -->`.

Example:

```
<!-- This is a comment explaining the code -->

<head></head>
```

Now that we discussed how to write HTML properly, let's explore what are some common HTML elements that all novice front-end web developers should know.

Important HTML Tags to Know

For novice front-end web developers, mastering common HTML tags is crucial to creating well-structured web pages. Here's a list of fundamental HTML tags every beginner should know:

1. Basic Structure Tags:

- `<html>`: The root element of an HTML document.
- `<head>`: Contains meta-information like title, styles, and scripts.
- `<body>`: Contains the content of the webpage (text, images, links, etc.).

---

2. Text and Content Tags:

- `<h1>` to `<h6>`: Header tags, with `<h1>` being the largest and usually the most important. Next is `<h2>` then `<h3>` next `<h4>`, `<h5>` and ending with `<h6>` as the smallest.
- `<p>`: Paragraph tag for blocks of text.
- `<strong>`: Boldens text for emphasis (also conveys semantic meaning for search engine optimization).

---

3. List Tags:

- `<ul>`: Unordered list (bulleted).
- `<ol>`: Ordered list (numbered).
- `<li>`: List item within `<ul>` or `<ol>`.

---

4. Link and Navigation Tags:

- `<a>`: Anchor tag for hyperlinks. Links to other pages or sections using the `href` attribute.
- `<nav>`: Defines a section for navigation links.

---

5. Media Tags:

- `<img>`: Embeds images using the `src` attribute to specify the image source.
- `<video>`: Embeds video content.
- `<audio>`: Embeds audio content.

---

6. Table Tags:

- `<table>`: Defines a table.

- `<tr>`: Table row.
- `<td>`: Table data (cell).
- `<th>`: Table header.

---

7. Form Tags:

- `<form>`: Creates an HTML form for user input.
- `<input>`: Defines an input field (e.g., text, checkbox, radio, etc.).
- `<button>`: Button for submitting forms or performing actions.
- `<label>`: Label for form elements.
- `<textarea>`: Multi-line text input field.

---

8. Grouping Tags:

- `<div>`: Division or container for structuring content.it is also called a *block-level element* because it is displayed on one line, and pushes non-block elements below or to the side of the block element.
- `<span>`: Inline container for styling or grouping small sections of text.
- `<id>`: this attribute is used to point to a specific style declaration in a style sheet (we will explore *stylesheets* in the *How CSS is added to HTML section* of the *CSS chapter*). It is also used by JavaScript (we will explore this in the *function section* of the *Javascript chapter*) to access and manipulate the element with the specific id.

---

10. Metadata Tags:

- `<meta>`: Provides metadata like character encoding, viewport settings, SEO tags. This tag is self closing.
- `<link>`: Links to external resources like stylesheets.

These tags form the foundation of HTML and are essential for structuring and presenting content on the web. Additionally, avoid deprecated elements. Some older HTML elements (like

`<font>`or `<center>`) are **deprecated** in modern HTML5 and should not be used. Use **CSS** for styling and layout instead.

Last Words About HTML

HTML (Hypertext Markup Language) is the skeleton of a webpage. It's the foundational language that defines the structure and content. Every element you see on a webpage—headings, paragraphs, images, links—are all defined by HTML. It creates the framework that tells browsers what content is on the page and how it's organized. By learning basic HTML, you've acquired the ability to structure content in a logical, hierarchical way.

Chapter 4: CSS (Cascading Style Sheets)

With **CSS (Cascading Style Sheets)**, you can control many aspects of the look and feel of an HTML webpage including text size, text color, font type, background color, borders, margins, etc. The unique functionality of CSS makes it one of the most widely used tools in web design and development today.

CSS Syntax

Just like HTML, to write CSS properly, there are a few things you should consider, following these syntax rules will ensure that your code is correct, easy to read, and can be used multiple times. Here are the syntax rules:

1. CSS Syntax Structure:

CSS consists of two main components: **selectors** and **declarations**.

- A **selector** identifies the HTML element you want to style.
- A **declaration** specifies the style to be applied.

Declarations are written inside **curly braces** `{ }` and consist of a **property** and a **value**, separated by a colon (`:`). Each declaration ends with a semicolon (`;`).

Basic Structure of CSS:

```
selector {
  property: value;
}
```

Example:

```
h1 {
  color: blue;
  font-size: 24px;
}
```

In this example:

- `h1` is the selector (it targets all `<h1>` elements).
- `color: blue;` is a declaration that changes the text color to blue.
- `font-size: 24px;` sets the font size to 24 pixels.

2. Selectors and Specificity:

- Different types of **Selectors** can also be used to determine which HTML elements get styled. Common types include:
  - **Type selectors** (e.g., `p`) target elements by name.
  - **Class selectors** (e.g., `.classname`) target elements with a specific class. The `.` is used to indicate that a class selector is being used.
  - **ID selectors** (e.g., `#idname`) target elements with a unique ID. The `#` is used to indicate that an ID selector is being used.
- **Specificity** determines which style is applied if multiple rules conflict:
  - IDs have higher specificity than classes, which have higher specificity than type selectors.
  - Inline styles `(style="...")` have the highest specificity. (we will explore inline styles in greater detail in the *How CSS is Added to HTML Section.*

---

3. Cascading and Inheritance:

- As I said earlier, CSS stands for **Cascading Style Sheets** because the styles "cascade" down. Because of this, if multiple rules apply to an element, the rule with the highest specificity or the rule declared last takes precedence. So if the rule is an ID it will take precedence over a Class. While a Class would take precedence over a Type.
- Some properties are **inherited** `(e.g., font-family)`, meaning they are passed down from parent elements to child elements. Others, like `margin` or `border`, are not inherited. We will explore these properties in greater detail in the *Common CSS Properties* section

---

4. Box Model:

- Every HTML element can be thought of as a **box**. Understanding the **box model** is crucial for layout. The box consists of **content**, **padding**, **border**, and **margin,** below I included an image of what the box model looks like, this will help you with using it:

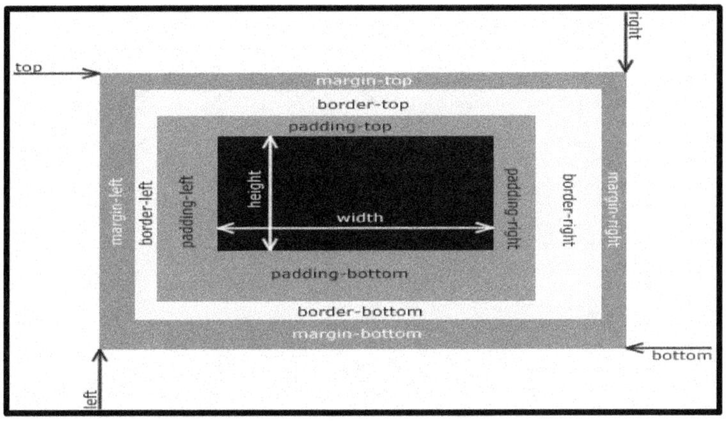

Cited:https://en.wikipedia.org/wiki/CSS_box_model

Example:

```
article {

  margin: 10px;

  padding: 20px;

  border: 1px solid black;

}
```

---

5. Units and Measurements:

- CSS uses a variety of units for lengths and sizes:
  - **Pixels** (`px`) are fixed units. For example, `10px`
  - **Percentages** (`%`) are relative to a parent container's size. E.g `10%`
  - **Ems** (`em`) and **rem** are relative units based on font size (useful for responsive design). E.g `10em` or `1rem`
- For responsive designs, relative units like `%`, `em`, and `rem` are preferred over fixed `px`.

---

6. Shorthand Properties:

- CSS has many **shorthand properties** that allow you to set multiple values at once, reducing the amount of code you write.

Example:

```
/* Longhand */

margin-top: 10px;

margin-right: 20px;

margin-bottom: 10px;

margin-left: 20px;


/* Shorthand */

margin: 10px 20px;
```

---

7. Pseudo Classes:

A **CSS pseudo-class** is a keyword added to selectors that specifies a special state of an element. Pseudo-classes are used to style elements based on dynamic factors like user interaction or position within the document, even though they might not be distinguishable through standard attributes.

For example, a pseudo-class can apply styles when:

- The user hovers over a link (`:hover`)
- A form input is focused (`:focus`)
- A link has been visited (`:visited`)
- The first child of an element is selected (`:first-child`)

Here's an example of using the `:hover` pseudo-class to change the color of a link when a user hovers over it:

```
a:hover {

  color: red;

}
```

In this case, when the user moves the mouse over a link, its color will change to red. Pseudo-classes are very useful for creating interactive designs and improving the user experience without requiring JavaScript.

---

8. Commenting:

- Comments in CSS are written with `/* */` and can help make your code more readable and easier to maintain.

Example:

```
/* This styles the heading */

h1 {

  color: blue; }
```

Common CSS Properties

Now that we explored CSS syntax in detail let's now go over other examples of common CSS properties you may encounter:

1. Color and Background:

- `color:` Sets the text color. **Example:** `{color: #333;}`

- `background-color:` Specifies the background color of an element. **Example:** `{background-color: #f5f5f5;}`

- `background-image:` Adds an image as the background of an element. Be sure to add url of the image you wish to add. **E.g;** `background-image: url('image.jpg');`

---

2. Typography:

- `font-family:` Specifies the font type.
  Example: `{font-family: 'Arial', sans-serif;}`

- `font-size:` Defines the size of the text.

Example: `{font-size: 16px;}`

- `font-weight`**:** Controls the boldness of the text.
  Example: `{font-weight: bold;}`

- `text-align`**:** Aligns text horizontally (left, center, right). **Example:** `{text-align: center;}`

- `line-height`**:** Controls the space between lines of text. **Example:** `{line-height: 1.5;}`

---

3. Spacing:

- `margin`**:** Defines the space outside the element.
  Example: `{margin: 20px;}`

- `padding`**:** Defines the space inside the element, between the content and the border.
  Example: `{padding: 15px;}`

---

4. Box Model:

- `width`**: and** `height`**:** Set the width and height of an element.
  Example:
  ```
  {width: 300px;
  height: 200px;
  }
  ```

- `border`**:** Adds a border around an element.
  Example: `{border: 1px solid #000;}`

- `border-radius`**:** sets the roundness of corners on the border
  Example: `{border-radius: 50px 20px;}`

- `box-shadow`**:** Adds shadow around an element.
  Example: `{border: 1px solid #000;}`

5. Positioning:

- `position:` Specifies the positioning method (static, relative, absolute, fixed).
  Example: `{position: relative;}`

- `top, right, bottom, left:` Offsets an element from its position.
  Example: `{top: 10px; left: 20px;}`

---

6. Display and Layout:

- `display:` Defines how an element is displayed (block, inline, inline-block, flex).
  Example:
  ```
  {display: block;
  display: flex;
  }
  ```

- `flex:` Enables flexbox layout properties for easier element alignment.
  Example: `{display: flex; justify-content: space-between;}`

- `overflow:` Controls how overflowed content is handled (visible, hidden, scroll).
  Example: `{overflow: hidden;}`

---

7. Visibility:

- `visibility:` Controls the visibility of an element (visible, hidden).
  Example: `{visibility: hidden;}`

- `opacity:` Sets the opacity (transparency) of an element.
  css
  Example: `{opacity: 0.5;}`

---

8. Hover Effects:

- `:hover:` Adds styles to an element when the mouse hovers over it.

Example: `a:hover { color: red;}`

Mobile Responsive Design

Producing websites that work seamlessly across mobile devices is now a requirement for a skilled developer in this age. The reason being, search engines only want to send users to websites that are "Mobile responsive".

This matters greatly for SEO, and again to be a great web developer you should definitely learn SEO. So reading this section will help you do it. Let's get into it;

1. Fluid Layouts:

- **Use Relative Units**: Instead of fixed units like `px` , use flexible units like percentages `(%)`, `em` , `rem` , or viewport-based units (`vw`, `vh`) for width, margin, padding, etc. This helps elements adapt to different screen sizes.

Example:
```
.container {

    width: 80%; /* Adapts to the size of the viewport */

}
```

---

2. Media Queries:

- **Adjust Layout Based on Screen Size**: Use media queries to apply different styles for various screen widths. This allows you to design for specific device sizes (mobile, tablet, desktop).

Example:
```
@media only screen and (max-width: 768px) {

    .container {

        width: 100%;
```

```
        padding: 10px;
    }
}
```

---

3. Mobile-First Approach:

- **Design for Small Screens First**: Start by designing for mobile devices, then use media queries to scale up for larger screens. This ensures that the essential content is optimized for smaller, more restrictive devices.

Example:

```
/* Default (mobile-first) */

body { font-size: 16px; }


/* For tablets and small desktops */

@media (min-width: 768px) and (max-width: 1024px)

{ body { font-size: 18px; }


/* For large desktops and up */

@media (min-width: 1025px)

{ body { font-size: 20px; } }
```

---

4. Flexible Grid Systems:

- **CSS Grid or Flexbox**: Use these layout systems to create flexible and adaptive grid structures that rearrange themselves based on screen size.

  Below I include an image that I cited showing the difference between a Flexbox and CSS Grid. As you can see the Flexbox is more "one-dimensional" this is for more archaic, static web pages. But with a grid, you can create dynamic layouts that adjust to different screen sizes, this is going to be more important for web app designing.

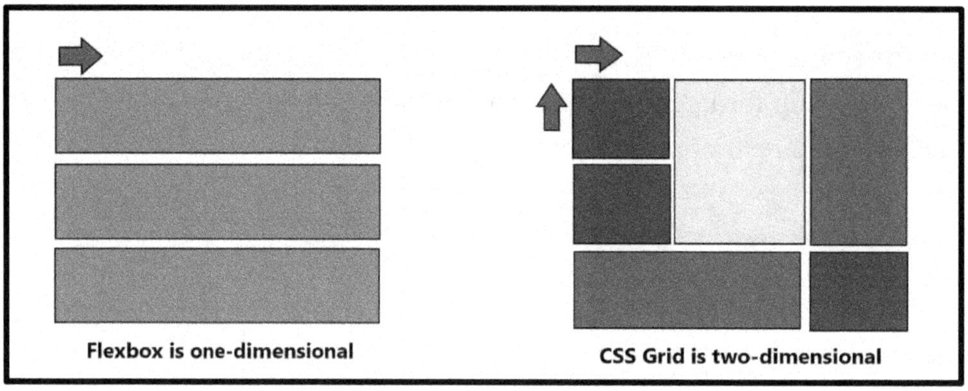

Cited:https://www.linkedin.com/pulse/revolutionizing-web-layouts-impact-flexbox-css-grid-razal-kabeer-qr0kf/

Flexbox Example:

```
.container {
    display: flex;
    flex-wrap: wrap;
}
.item {
    flex: 1 1 100%;
}
@media (min-width: 600px) {
```

```
    .item {
        flex: 1 1 50%;
    }
}
```

CSS Grid Example:

```
.grid {
    display: grid;
    grid-template-columns: 1fr;
}
@media (min-width: 768px) {
    .grid {
        grid-template-columns: 1fr 1fr;
    }
}
```

---

5. Viewport Meta Tag:

- **Set the Viewport for Mobile Devices**: Use the viewport meta tag in the HTML to ensure the browser adjusts the layout properly for mobile screens. If you recall from the *HTML Chapter* this tag is pivotal to having an optimal search engine performance as well, so don't forget it.

Example:

```
<meta name="viewport" content="width=device-width, initial-scale=1.0">
```

---

6. Responsive Images:

- **Use** `max-width` **for Images**: Ensure images resize proportionally by setting a `max-width` of 100% so they don't overflow their container.

Example:

```
img {

    max-width: 100%;

    height: auto;

}
```

---

7. Hide/Show Content:

- **Display or Hide Elements**: Sometimes, you may need to hide certain elements on smaller screens or show alternative content. You can use media queries to control visibility.

Example:

```
.desktop-only {

    display: none;

}

@media (min-width: 1024px) {

    .desktop-only {

        display: block;
```

```
    }
}
```

---

8. Test on Different Devices:

- **Cross-Device Testing**: Always test your site on different devices or use responsive design tools in browsers to ensure your styles work well across different screen sizes.

---

9. Touch-Friendly Elements:

- **Larger Clickable Areas**: Ensure that buttons, links, and interactive elements are large enough and spaced adequately for touch screens. Search engines like Google recommend a minimum touch target size of **48x48 pixels**.

---

10. CSS Frameworks (Optional):

- **Use CSS Frameworks**: "CSS frameworks" come with built-in responsive design utilities, grid systems, and pre-designed components that can help accelerate development. However, it's beneficial to understand the underlying principles before relying heavily on frameworks.

Final Thoughts

Understanding these properties will help you as a beginner create well-structured and visually appealing websites, while also providing a solid foundation to build more advanced designs. In the next section, we are going to explore the different ways in which CSS can be added to an HTML document.

How CSS is Added to HTML

CSS can be added to an HTML document generally in three ways: *inline, external,* or *internal*. Each way has pros and cons.

Inline CSS

For CSS to be added inline, the *style attribute* `style=""` or a special modifier that allows the CSS file to be referenced is added to the HTML tag or element.
Here's an example from:

```
<h1 style="color:blue;">insert text here</h1>
```

As you can see the code snippet includes the HTML element that is to be styled, this is also known as the *selector*. In this case, we are styling the **`<h1>`** element. Then an equal sign `=` and quotation marks `""` are added to show that you are including a *declaration* that tells the computer to use the style defined in quotation marks.

Next, a *property* is added, which is the name of the style you want to use.

In the code example above, the property is `color` (change the font color).

The property is then followed by a colon **:**, then the *value* or what you want to change the element to.

For color, I wrote `blue`. Lastly, you end the declaration statement with a semicolon `;`

Also as you can see the style modifier is only added to the opening tag `<h1>`, this modifier should never be added to the closing tag `</h1>`

Pros and Cons

Here are some pros and cons of inline CSS implementation:

Pros:

- Useful for overriding default styling
- Has a higher specificity than any CSS selector (recall this information from the *CSS syntax section*; inline styles are more specific than **ID**, which is more specific than **Class**, which is more specific than **Type**. Also note this can be a Con because it can override more general styling and external stylesheets.

Cons:

- Not an easy way to apply styling for the whole page, especially if it's large
- Has a higher specificity than any CSS selector which can override external stylesheets

- Hard to manage and maintain.

External CSS

CSS can also be applied through an *external* file with the **.CSS** extension and then load it within a web page with an `<link>` HTML tag, and a `rel` and `href` attribute added to the link tag.

Here's an example:

```
<head>
  <link rel="stylesheet" href="styles.css">
</head>
```

As you can see the code; `<link rel="stylesheet" href="styles.css">` was nested in `<head>` tag.

The `<link>` tag indicates that a file is being called or located from another document. The `rel` attribute is used to indicate what type of file is to be requested, in this case a `stylesheet`. Then the `href` attribute indicates the name of the stylesheet file in this case, `styles.css`.

You may be wondering, what does the `styles.css` file look like?

Here's a `styles.css` code snippet:

```
h1 {
  color: red;
}
```

In the code snippet, you can also see the HTML element that is to be styled. Again, in this case, the selector is added, `<h1>` element, followed by curly brackets `{}` to indicate the start of the declaration. The `color` property is again added.

Then the property is again followed by a colon `:` then the "value" or what you want the property to be is added. For color, I added `red` and then ended the declaration statement with a semicolon `;`

Now, here are the pros and cons of using external CSS:

Pros and Cons

Pros:

- All styles are stored in one separate file, making it easier to manage and maintain;
- Ability to include multiple different files if needed;
- Comments can be added to be interpretation easier for different developers
- The CSS file can be minified meaning decreased size in bytes. (This matters for SEO)

Cons:

- Linking external files creates render-blocking content which affects the rate and speed that Search engines can crawl and index web pages. Additionally, this can lead to a poor user experience because it may take visitors longer to access the website (Again this matters for SEO).
- May contain styles that are not used on a particular page, thus loading unused code. Which again can slow the rate and speed at which the website can be accessed and crawled by search engines.

Internal CSS

Lastly, we have internal CSS. Internal CSS is deployed using the `<style>` element nested in the `<head>` tag, again if you recall the `<head>` tag is generally where non-viewable/ non-interactive web elements are stored.

Next, nested in the `<style>` element is the *selector* or the element name that is to be styled is then included, in this case, it is the H2 tag `<h2>` again followed by curly brackets `{ }` to indicate the start of a declaration and then the property you want to style.

Here's an example:

```
<head>
     <style>
          H2 {
               Color: green;
               font-family: times new roman

               font-weight: bold;
               }
     </style>
</head>
```

In the code example, there are two new properties: `font-family` (changes the font type), and `font-weight` (Changes the thinness or thickness of the font).

The declaration is then followed by a colon `:`, then the value or what you want the property to be is added.

For `color`, I wrote `green`, for `font-family`, I wrote `times new roman`, and for `font-weight`, I wrote `bold`, to indicate I want the font to be thick. You end the declaration statement with a semicolon `;`

Now, let's review the pros and cons:

Pros and Cons

Pros:

- Useful for overriding default styling;
- Can be turned on and off with JavaScript;
- Can be used to contain default minimum styling if the main stylesheet is being loaded asynchronously.

Cons:

- Not a very convenient way to apply styling for the whole page, especially if it's large;

- Hard to manage and maintain.

Last Words About CSS

CSS (Cascading Style Sheets) is the design language of the web. While HTML provides the structure, CSS is what gives a website its visual presentation, transforming plain content into a visually engaging experience. Everything from colors, fonts, spacing, and layout is controlled by CSS, allowing you to craft a unique look and feel for each webpage. By learning basic CSS, you've acquired the skills to style and enhance web content in ways that improve both aesthetics and usability.

Chapter 5: JavaScript

JavaScript is a versatile, high-level programming language used to create interactive, and dynamic effects on a web page, that happen based on user interactions like clicks, typing, scrolling, and more.

These effects can be things such as *pop-up ads*, animations, and much more. If you've ever used a form that instantly warns you about incorrect data without refreshing the page or a button that opens a dropdown menu, that's JavaScript at work.

Syntax

JavaScript Syntax or the unique set of rules the code must follow in order to be interpreted correctly by the browser. There are several key parts to JavaScript Syntax.

- First, it is case-sensitive, meaning changing the case of a letter can change the syntax of the code. For example, ***`FirstName`*** is not interpreted the same as ***`firstname`*** the browser would instead interpret these pieces of code as two different variables.

- Also, JavaScript uses a **unicode character set** which means developers have access to letters, numbers, and symbols from any language.

- Additionally, JavaScript statements are sometimes ended with a **semicolon** `;` but this practice has fallen out of style in the programming community.

JavaScript syntax definitely goes much deeper than this, but these are some of the basics. In the next chapter, we will cover the more intricate aspects of JavaScript Syntax.

JavaScript Syntax in Detail

Here are the additional key components of JavaScript syntax;**Variables, Data Types, Operators, Statements**, **Expressions**, **Functions**, **DOM Manipulation, Events, Conditional Statements**, **Loops,** and **Comments**. Understanding this is pivotal to being able to code JavaScript effectively.

Values

In JavaScript, **Values** can be thought of as pieces or chunks of information that are assigned to different numbers or pieces of text.

In JavaScript syntax, two of the most common values are **Literals** and **Variables**.

- **Fixed values** - Literals
- **Changeable values** - Variables

Literals

Fixed values are also referred to as **Literals**, they are called "fixed values" because they are values that generally are not changed, once they are declared they remain as such. They can be **Numbers** written either with or without decimals like:

```
9.20
```

```
9001
```

Or **Strings** which are text, written within double or single quotes:

```
"John Doe"
```

```
'John Doe'
```

Both types of values can be used to store pieces of information. There are additional *Data Types* like **Boolean, Array, Objects,** and **symbols,** which are standalone entities or things with their own identity and properties. We will explore *Data Types* in more detail in its own section.

Each of these can be used to represent values as well, but Fixed values and strings are the most simplistic, and can help you establish a foundation for exploring more intricate values in the future.

Variables

As I mentioned**, Variables** are changeable values. A Variable can be declared using `var`, `let`, and `const` keywords, according to:

- `var` is a more archaic way to define a JavaScript variable. It has fallen out of use because it can cause confusion with other JavaScript keywords, and it has limited usage due to scoping issues.

- `let` removes the confusion and error of `var`. It is the new and recommended way of declaring variables in JavaScript.

- `const` is used to declare a constant variable that cannot be changed once assigned a value.

Variables can also be thought of as digital containers for holding Literal values. Revisiting the last example here are variables written with numbers:

```
var x = 5;

let y = 6;

const z = x + y;
```

As you can see, the keywords `var,` `let`, and `const`, are used to designate variables. Additionally in the code snippet; **operators** are used to perform mathematical and logical operations between variables, as you can see the operators = and + were used. I will explain this concept and the code snippet in more detail in the next section.

Data Types

As I mentioned, in addition to Numbers, Literal Values and Variables can be represented by different *Data Types* like:

1. String:

A sequence of characters, used to represent text.

Example:

```
let greeting = "Hello, World!";
console.log(greeting); // Output: Hello, World!
```

---

2. Number:

Represents both integer and floating-point numbers, i.e. digits like 123

Example:

```
let age = 30;
let pi = 3.14;
console.log(age); // Output: 30
console.log(pi);  // Output: 3.14
```

---

3. Boolean:

Represents logical entities, having only two values: `true` or `false`.

Example:

```
let isDeveloper = true;
console.log(isDeveloper); // Output: true
```

---

4. Array:

An ordered list of values, or that can be referenced by name i.e. a collection of items (indexed elements).

Example:

```
let colors = ["red", "green", "blue"];
console.log(colors[1]); // Output: green
```

---

5. Object:

A collection of key-value pairs.

Example:

```
let person = {
  name: "Alice",
  age: 25,
  isStudent: false
};
```

```
console.log(person.name); // Output: Alice
```

---

6. Symbol:

A unique and immutable primitive value, often used as a key in object properties.

Example:

```
let sym = Symbol("uniqueKey");
let obj = {
  [sym]: "value"
};
console.log(obj[sym]); // Output: value
```

---

7. Undefined:

A variable that has been declared but not yet assigned a value.

Example:

```
let notAssigned;
console.log(notAssigned); // Output: undefined
```

---

8. Null:

Represents the intentional absence of any object value.

Example:

```
let emptyValue = null;
console.log(emptyValue); // Output: null
```

Operators

An **Operator** is a symbol that is used to perform a mathematical or logical operation between variables or values.

Here's the code snippet example I referenced in the *Variable section*:

```
var x = 5;

var y = 6;

var z = x + y;
```

The symbol `=` is used to represent the **assignment operator** which is used to assign values to a specific symbol. In this case, it is used to show that the **letter X** is equal to 5 and **letter Y** is equal to 6.

Also the assignment operator is used in conjunction with the **addition operator** `+` to show that the **letter *Z*** is equal to the sum of letters **X** and **Y**.

There are other *arithmetic operators* such as:

Arithmetic operators

1. Subtraction (-):

Description: Subtracts the right-hand operand from the left-hand operand.

Example:

```
let result = 10 - 5; // result is 5
```

Explanation: Here, `10 - 5` equals `5`. The `-` operator simply subtracts the right-hand operand value of `5` from the left-hand operand value of `10`.

---

2. Multiplication Operator (*)

Description: The multiplication operator is used to multiply two numbers.

Example:

```
let a = 6;

let b = 4;

let result = a * b; // Multiplies 6 by 4

console.log(result); // Output: 24
```

Explanation: Here, `6 * 4` equals `24`. The `*` operator simply multiplies the two numbers on either side of it.

---

3. Division (/):

Description: Divides the left-hand operand by the right-hand operand.

Example:
```
let result = 10 / 2; // result is 5
```

Explanation: Here, `10 / 2` equals `5`. The `/` operator simply divides the left-hand operand `10` by the right-hand operand `2`.

---

4. Modulus (%):

Description: Returns the remainder of the division between two numbers.

Example:
```
let result = 10 % 3; // result is 1
```

Explanation: Here, `10 % 3` equals `1`. The `%` operator simply divides the left-hand operand `10` by the right-hand operand `3`. Because `10` divided by `3` gives a remainder of `1` the answer is `1`

Comparison Operators

Comparison operators help you perform logical comparisons in your JavaScript code, allowing you to control the flow of execution based on conditions. Here they are:

1. Equality (==)

Description: Compares two values for equality after converting them to a common type (type coercion).

Example:

```
console.log(5 == '5'); // true
```

Here, the string '5' is converted to a number before comparison.

---

2. Inequality (!=)

Description: Compares two values for inequality after type coercion.

Example:

```
console.log(5 != '6'); // true
```

The values are not equal, so it returns true.

---

3. Strict Equality (===)

Description: Compares two values for equality without type conversion (no coercion).

Example:

```
console.log(5 === '5'); // false
```

Here, the comparison fails because the types (number vs. string) are different.

---

4. Strict Inequality (!==)

Description: Compares two values for inequality without type conversion.

Example:

```
console.log(5 !== '5'); // true
```

The values are not equal due to different types, so it returns true.

---

5. Less Than (<)

Description: Checks if the left operand is less than the right operand.

Example:
```
console.log(5 < 10); // true
```

---

6. Greater Than (>)

Description: Checks if the left operand is greater than the right operand.

Example:
```
console.log(10 > 5); // true
```

---

7. Less Than or Equal To (<=)

Description: Checks if the left operand is less than or equal to the right operand.

Example:
```
console.log(5 <= 5); // true
```

---

8. Greater Than or Equal To (>=)

Description: Checks if the left operand is greater than or equal to the right operand.

Example:
```
console.log(10 >= 5); // true
```

Summary

- `==` and `!=`: Perform type coercion.
- `===` and `!==`: No type coercion; strict checks.

- `<`, `>`, `<=`, `>=`: Compare numerical values.

These operators help you perform logical comparisons in your JavaScript code, allowing you to control the flow of execution based on conditions.

Logical Operators

Logical operators are used to combine or invert boolean values. The three main logical operators are:

Logical AND (`&&`):

Description: This operator returns `true` if both operands are true.

Example:

```
const a = true;

const b = false;

const result = a && b; // result is false
```

Explanation: Here, result is `false` because both `a` and `b` must be true for the result to be `true`.

Logical OR (`||`):

Description: This operator returns `true` if at least one of the operands is true.

Example:

```
const a = true;

const b = false;
```

```
const result = a || b; // result is true
```

Explanation: In this case, result is `true` because `a` is true, so the overall expression evaluates to true.

Logical NOT (`!`):

Description: This operator inverts the boolean value of its operand.

Example:

```
const a = true;
const result = !a; // result is false
```

Explanation: Here, result is `false` because the NOT operator flips `true` to `false`.

Combining Logical Operators

You can also combine these operators to create more complex conditions:

```
const x = 5;
const y = 10;
const isGreater = (x > 3) && (y < 15); // isGreater is true
const isEither = (x < 3) || (y > 15); // isEither is false
const notTrue = !(x === 5); // notTrue is false
```

Explanation: In this example:

`isGreater is true` because both conditions are true.

`isEither is false` because neither condition is true.

`notTrue is false` because the expression `x === 5` is true, and the NOT operator inverts it.

These logical operators are fundamental in controlling the flow of your code, especially in conditional statements.

typeof Operator

The `typeof` operator in JavaScript is used to determine the type of a variable or an expression. It returns a string indicating the type. Here are some examples along with explanations:

Example 1: Basic Types

```
console.log(typeof "Hello, World!"); // "string"

console.log(typeof 42);              // "number"

console.log(typeof true);              // "boolean"

console.log(typeof undefined);         // "undefined"

console.log(typeof null);              // "object" (this is a
known quirk in JavaScript)
```

Explanation:

- `typeof "Hello, World!"` returns `"string"` because it's a string value.
- `typeof 42` returns `"number"` since 42 is a numeric value.
- `typeof true` returns `"boolean"` because it's a boolean value.
- `typeof undefined` returns `"undefined"` when a variable has been declared but not assigned a value.
- `typeof null` returns `"object"` due to a historical bug in JavaScript.

Example 2: Complex Types

```
console.log(typeof { name: "Alice", age: 30 }); // "object"

console.log(typeof [1, 2, 3]);                // "object"
(arrays are also objects)

console.log(typeof function() {});             // "function"

console.log(typeof new Date());                // "object"
```

Explanation:

- `typeof { name: "Alice", age: 30 }` returns `"object"` because it's an object literal.
- `typeof [1, 2, 3]` returns `"object"` because arrays are technically objects in JavaScript.
- `typeof function() {}` returns `"function"` since functions are first-class objects.
- `typeof new Date()` returns `"object"` because a Date is also an object.

Example 3: Checking for Specific Types

```
let variable = "Hello";


if (typeof variable === "string") {

    console.log("It's a string!");

} else {

    console.log("It's not a string.");

}
```

Explanation: In this example, we check if `variable` is of type `"string"` using the `typeof` operator. If it is, we log "It's a string!". In this case the variable is `"Hello";` which is a string because it's letters so the console should log `It's a string!`

Summary

The `typeof` operator is useful for type checking and debugging, allowing developers to understand the data types they are working with in their code.

Bitwise XOR Operator

The ^ operator is a bitwise XOR (exclusive OR) operator. It compares two numbers on a bit level (binary) and returns 1 when the bits are different and 0 when they are the same.

Example:

```
let num1 = 5;   // Binary: 101

let num2 = 3;   // Binary: 011

let result = num1 ^ num2; // XOR: 110 (6 in decimal)

console.log(result); // Output: 6
```

Explanation:

- 5 in binary is `101`
- 3 in binary is `011`
- XOR compares the bits:
  - 1 ^ 0 = 1
  - 0 ^ 1 = 1
  - 1 ^ 0 = 0
- So the result is `110` (which is 6 in decimal).

Bitwise XOR can be useful in programming for various tasks, like:

- Finding differences between numbers.
- Swapping values without a temporary variable.
- Creating checksums for data verification.

As you can see, there is an operator to represent virtually every mathematical or logical operation.

Statements

Statements are lines of code that instruct the browser to perform a specific task or function. They are essentially a sequence of operators, values and expressions that are grouped together meant to be interpreted in a specific order or fashion.

Here's an example of a statement:

```
let x, y, z;

x = 7;

y = 3;

z = x + y;
```

As you can see the statement is used to instruct the browser on how to solve `Z = X + Y`, which based on the instruction should be `10`.

Expressions

An expression is an example of a *statement*, it is a combination of values, variables, and operators.

Essentially it is a sequence of calculations that lead to a unique value, like a number sentence such as; `5 + 3` = the value of `8` or `2*3` = the value of `6`.

Examples of expressions include arithmetic operations (you may recall these from the ***operators section***) such as `+` addition, `-` subtraction, `*` multiplication, and `/` division, as well as `&&` logical and `==` comparison operations.

As you can see from the examples, the symbols used in each expression are the same as the JavaScript operators mentioned earlier.

Functions

Functions are a code snippet that includes "procedures" or a set of statements and expressions that are grouped together for a specific purpose or to perform a task. Essentially they are meant to be used over and over again as opposed to creating a new function for every use.

Here's an example:

```
function toCelsius(fahrenheit) {
  return (5/9) * (fahrenheit-32);
}
document.getElementById("demo").innerHTML = toCelsius(77);
```

The function includes several key parts:

```
function toCelsius(fahrenheit)
```

This statement identifies the function or procedure to be completed, in this case, the procedure is to convert Fahrenheit to Celsius.

Next part of the code snippet:

```
{
  return (5/9) * (fahrenheit-32);
}
```

This statement indicates the sequence of expressions to be completed in order to `return` the answer to the question.

Essentially the statement is saying to convert a Fahrenheit measurement to Celsius, the following steps must first be completed; Divide `5/9`, and take the inputted Fahrenheit measurement minus `-` `32`. Then take the result of these two expressions and multiply `*` them. As you can see the order in which these operations are performed is important in order to return the correct answer.

Then the last statement:

```
document.getElementById("demo").innerHTML = toCelsius(77);
```

Is instructing the computer to show the answer to the function on the user's screen via HTML more specifically as an HTML tag with the `id "demo"` (We will explore *DOM (Dynamic Object Model)* manipulation) in the next section.

The last part of the statement `toCelsius(77);` between the parentheses `()` is where the programmer would input the Fahrenheit number they wish to be converted.

In this case, the Fahrenheit number inputted was `77F`. So the result should be `25C`.

Again as you can see functions are great because they allow you to write reusable pieces of code. Instead of repeating yourself, you define a function and use it multiple times throughout your program.

DOM (Document Object Model) Manipulation

The **Document Object Model (DOM)** represents the structure of a webpage as a tree of objects. Each element on the page is part of this tree. JavaScript allows you to access and manipulate the DOM, which enables dynamic updates to the HTML content. You can use the graphic I included below from wikipedia to help you with making sense of the DOM.

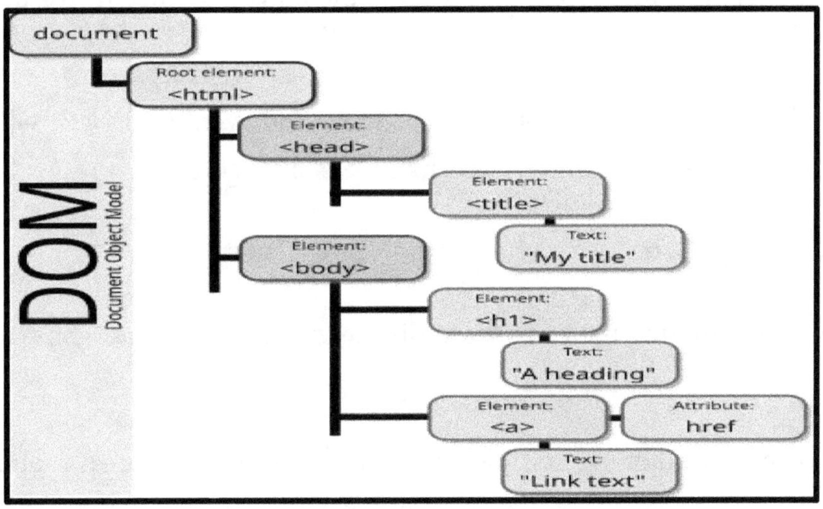

Cited From: https://en.wikipedia.org/wiki/Document_Object_Model

As you can recall from the *functions section* with the Fahrenheit to Celsius function, we used DOM manipulation to show the answer to the function on the user's screen via HTML more specifically as an HTML tag with the `id "demo"`

Here are some more additional things you can do with DOM manipulation. For example, you can:

- Change the content of an element.
- Modify the styles dynamically.
- Add or remove elements from the page.

Let's look at another example of DOM manipulation in action:

```
document.getElementById("heading").innerHTML = "New Heading Text";
```

This line of JavaScript will change the content of an HTML element with the ID `heading` to `"New Heading Text"`. As you can see DOM manipulation is an excellent way to bring static webpages to life.

Events

An **Event** is a signal or alert that is triggered when users interact with an HTML element on a webpage.

Essentially events are actions or occurrences that happen in the browser, like clicking a button, hovering over a link, or submitting a form. JavaScript allows you to "listen" for these events and respond to them.

Here's an example of an HTML code snippet that just uses the event `onlick` which tells the browser to trigger an event when a button `<button>` is clicked on:

```
<button onclick="displayDate()">The time is?</button>
```

This particular event is instructing the browser to display a date, when the `button` is clicked on.

JavaScript can also listen for other events, such as `mouseover`, `keypress`, and `load`. As you can see, Events are a great way to build interactive web pages.

Conditional Statements

Conditional statements determine whether or not pieces of code can run, or if it is true or false. Essentially, you use them to execute code only if certain conditions are met.

There are three main types of conditional statements:

`if` statements: where if a condition is <u>true</u> it is used to specify execution for a block of code.

`else` statements: where if the same condition is <u>false</u> it specifies the execution for a block of code.

`else if` statements: this specifies a new test if the first condition is false.

Here's a code snippet example:

```
let num = 7;

if (num > 10) {
  console.log("The number is greater than 10.");
} else if (num > 5) {
  console.log("The number is greater than 5 but less than or equal
to 10.");
} else {
  console.log("The number is less than or equal to 5.");
}
```

The `let num = 7` indicates that the variable `num` will be assigned a value of `7`.

The `if` statement; `if (num > 10)` checks whether the value of the `num` variable is greater than `10`. If the statement is `true` then the text: `("The number is greater than 10.")` will be displayed on the user's console.

Since `num` is actually `7`, this condition is `false`, so the next statement `else if (num > 5)` will be executed instead.

If the statement is `true` for this piece of code, then the text: `("The number is greater than 5 but less than or equal to 10.")` will be displayed on the user's console.

But if the answer is `false`, then `else` statement is executed; if the value of `num` is less than `5`, then the console will instead log: `("The number is less than or equal to 5.")`

As you can see, Conditional statements are a significant part of JavaScript programming and are a great way to make the code more dynamic and responsive to user input or other changing conditions.

Loops

In JavaScript, loops are used to repeatedly execute a block of code as long as a specified condition is true. This allows you to automate repetitive tasks, iterate over data structures like arrays, or perform actions a set number of times. There are several types of loops in JavaScript:

1. `for` Loop

The `for` loop is commonly used when you know in advance how many times you want to iterate.

```
for (let i = 0; i < 5; i++) {

  console.log(i); // Output: 0, 1, 2, 3, 4

}
```

- **Initialization**: `let i = 0;` — This runs once at the start of the loop.
- **Condition**: `i < 5;` — The loop continues as long as this condition is true.
- **Increment/Update**: `i++` — This runs after each iteration.

---

2. `while` Loop

The `while` loop repeats as long as a specified condition is true.

```
let i = 0;

while (i < 5) {

  console.log(i);
```

```
  i++;
}
```

---

3. `do...while` Loop

The `do...while` loop is similar to the `while` loop, but it ensures that the loop runs at least once, even if the condition is initially false.

```
let i = 0;
do {
  console.log(i);
  i++;
} while (i < 5);
```

---

4. `for...of` Loop

This loop iterates over iterable objects like arrays, strings, or sets.

```
let array = [10, 20, 30];
for (let value of array) {
  console.log(value); // Output: 10, 20, 30
}
```

---

5. `for...in` Loop

This loop iterates over the keys of an object or an array's indices.

```
let obj = { a: 1, b: 2, c: 3 };
for (let key in obj) {
```

```
  console.log(key); // Output: a, b, c
}
```

Key Points:

- `for` is for a defined number of iterations.
- `while` is for conditional looping until the condition is false.
- `for...of` iterates over values of an iterable.
- `for...in` iterates over keys (properties or indices).

These looping mechanisms help to perform repetitive tasks efficiently in JavaScript.

Comments

To inform others about the instructions of the JavaScript code, developers are able to write **Comments**.

The comments also give the observer info on the **semantics** or the meaning of the code. To indicate a single line comment, a user inputs double slashes `//`

Also any code that is between the slashes; `/` and `/` is treated as a comment also.

Lastly, a comment can also be used to stop a line of code from being executed, for testing purposes.

Here's an example of comments in action:

Code Snippet A: `let x = 5;    // I will be executed`

Code Snippet B: `// x = 6;    I will NOT be executed`

As you can see from the example, **Code Snippet A** will be executed, because the expression `let x = 5;` is included before the double slashes `//`. While **Code Snippet B** will not be executed because the expression `x = 6;` is not included before the double slashes.

Overall, JavaScript comments are pretty straight forward, and they are good to use when you need to provide information about what the code is being used for. Also if you want to stop a line of code from being executed so you can test the code.

In the next section we are going to explore the different ways in which JavaScript can be added to an HTML document. This will help you will be able to implement JavaScript yourself.

How JavaScript is Added to HTML

JavaScript can be implemented on web pages in one of three ways:

1. Inline
2. External
3. Internally

Again, each has its own pros and cons.

Internal JavaScript

If JavaScript is written directly in an HTML document, a `<script>` tag in the `<head>` section of the document with the `language` and `type` attributes added indicates the code has been added.

Here's an example of a series of functions:

```
<head>
     <script language = "javascript" type = "text/javascript">
(function (w, d, s, l, i) {
        w[l] = w[l] || [];
        w[l].push({ "gtm.start": new Date().getTime(), event:
"gtm.js" });
        var f = d.getElementsByTagName(s)[0],
          j = d.createElement(s),
          dl = l != "dataLayer" ? "&l=" + l : "";
        j.async = true;
        j.src = "https://www.googletagmanager.com/gtm.js?id=" +
i + dl;
        f.parentNode.insertBefore(j, f);
```

```
        })(window, document, "script", "dataLayer", "GTM-KVL636G");

    </script>
</head>
```

As you can see the code snippet is *nested* inside the `<head>` tags and the *`language`* and `type` attributes were added to the `<script>` tag to indicate that a JavaScript code snippet is being added.

The "code" nested in the `<script>` tag is an example of a *tracking pixel* which is a piece of JavaScript code used to track a webpage user's actions on the page.

Pros and Cons

Pros:

- Generally takes up less space

Cons:

- If in the `<head>` section it can slow down the webpage (render-blocking)
- May be harder to maintain and reuse code

External JavaScript

The code can also be loaded through an *external* file with the `.js` extension and then loading it within the page with again a `<script>` tag, and an [`src`] attribute added to the script tag, here's an example:

```
<body>
    <script src="name of file.js"></script>
</body>
```

The code does not necessarily need to be nested in the `<head>` tag. In this case, the code is being loaded from the `<body>` section of the HTML document.

Here are some pros and cons of external JavaScript:

Pros and Cons

Pros:

- Easy to reuse code.
- Easier to read
- Easier to compress and minify

Cons:

- The browser has to make an extra HTTP request to get the `.js` code.
- Code can be downloaded using the URL of the `.js` file. This can help coders to steal your code easily.
- If two `.js` files are dependent on one another, then a failure in one file may affect the execution of the other dependent file.
- A small change to a common `.js` file may cause unexpected results in some of the HTML files.

Inline JavaScript

Lastly, you can add the JavaScript code *inline* or directly inside an HTML tag, and then add **attributes** to the tag that trigger an action when interacted with such as:

- `onclick` (when the object is clicked on by the user)
- `onmouseover` (when the user moves their mouse)
- `onkeypress` (when the user presses a specific key on their keyboard)
- `onload` (when the user loads the webpage), etc.

These are also considered to be examples of **JavaScript Events** (recall the *Events section*)

Here's an example:

```
<button onclick="alert('Hello World!')">Click Me</button>
```

As you can see the attribute `onclick` was added with the action to show a display box with the text "Hello world" when the button is clicked on.

Here are the Pros and Cons for this method:

Pros and Cons

Pros:

- Generally takes up less space

Cons:

- Harder to maintain code
- Difficult to reuse code for other projects
- Unable to be *cached* or saved for future use by Web Browsers

Last Words About JavaScript

JavaScript is an essential tool for every web developer. It allows you to go beyond static content and create engaging, interactive websites that respond to user input. Whether it's adding a simple button click event or building an entire web application, JavaScript is the key to unlocking dynamic functionality on the web. By learning JavaScript, you will be able to build the next great website.

Last Words

Now obviously learning and mastering each of these coding languages would take a long time, but I wanted to teach you at least the basics so that when you are building your site yourself or having other people help you, you are not lost. It is very easy to get taken advantage of when it comes to website building, so knowing the basics is always key.

That's why in the next chapter I give you a basic breakdown of how to create a website from scratch, so that even if you move to a CMS or have someone else build your site, you are not completely lost.

Chapter 6: Creating A Website From Scratch

Now that you have a solid comprehension of HTML, CSS, and JavaScript, now is the time to start thinking about do you want to create your website from scratch, or use a CMS (Content management system) to manage your content.

In the next chapter, I will talk about CMSs but for this one, let's talk about if you were to create your own. I think this is good as a great beginner project, but as you get better or become more serious, a CMS may be worth the investment.

Here's a quick start up guide for making a website from scratch. It's very basic so if you want more detail you can look it up on your own.

Step 1: Set Up Your Project

1. Create a new folder for your project.
2. Inside the folder, create these files:
   - `index.html` (Homepage)
   - `about.html` (Additional page)
   - `styles.css` (CSS for styling)
   - `script.js` (JavaScript for interactivity)

Step 2: Build the Basic HTML Structure

Homepage (`index.html`)

```
<!DOCTYPE html>

<html lang="en">

<head>

    <meta charset="UTF-8">

    <meta name="viewport" content="width=device-width, initial-scale=1.0">
```

```
    <title>My First Website</title>
    <link rel="stylesheet" href="styles.css">
</head>
<body>
    <header>
        <h1>Welcome to My Website</h1>
        <nav>
            <a href="index.html">Home</a> |
            <a href="about.html">About</a>
        </nav>
    </header>
    <main>
        <p>This is a simple website created with HTML, CSS, and JavaScript.</p>
        <button id="clickMe">Click Me</button>
        <p id="message"></p>

        <h2>Contact Us</h2>
        <form id="contactForm">
            <label for="name">Name:</label>
            <input type="text" id="name" required>
```

```
            <label for="email">Email:</label>
            <input type="email" id="email" required>
            <button type="submit">Submit</button>
        </form>
        <p id="formMessage"></p>
    </main>
    <script src="script.js"></script>
</body>
</html>
```

Step 3: Create an Additional Page (`about.html`)

```
<!DOCTYPE html>
<html lang="en">
<head>
    <meta charset="UTF-8">
    <meta name="viewport" content="width=device-width, initial-
scale=1.0">
    <title>About Us</title>
    <link rel="stylesheet" href="styles.css">
</head>
<body>
    <header>
```

```
        <h1>About Us</h1>
        <nav>
            <a href="index.html">Home</a> |
            <a href="about.html">About</a>
        </nav>
    </header>
    <main>
        <p>This is the about page of our website.</p>
    </main>
</body>
</html>
```

Step 4: Style the Website with CSS (`styles.css`)

```
body {
    font-family: Arial, sans-serif;
    text-align: center;
    margin: 50px;
    background-color: #f4f4f4;
}

header {
```

```
    background: #333;
    color: white;
    padding: 20px;
}

nav {
    margin-top: 10px;
}

nav a {
    color: white;
    text-decoration: none;
    margin: 0 10px;
}

button {
    padding: 10px 20px;
    font-size: 16px;
    margin-top: 10px;
    cursor: pointer;
```

```
}

button:hover {
    background-color: #555;
    color: white;
}

form {
    display: flex;
    flex-direction: column;
    align-items: center;
    margin-top: 20px;
}

input {
    padding: 8px;
    margin: 5px;
    width: 200px;
}
```

Step 5: Add More Interactivity with JavaScript (`script.js`)

```
// Button Click Event

document.getElementById("clickMe").addEventListener("click",
function() {

    document.getElementById("message").textContent = "You
clicked the button!";

});


// Form Submission Event

document.getElementById("contactForm").addEventListener("submit"
, function(event) {

    event.preventDefault(); // Prevent page reload

    const name = document.getElementById("name").value;

    const email = document.getElementById("email").value;


    if (name && email) {

        document.getElementById("formMessage").textContent =
`Thank you, ${name}! We'll contact you at ${email}.`;

    } else {

        document.getElementById("formMessage").textContent =
"Please fill in all fields.";

    }

});
```

Step 6: Run Your Website

1. Open `index.html` in a web browser.
2. Click the button to see a message.
3. Fill out the form and submit it to see dynamic text updates.
4. Click the **About** page link to navigate to another page.

Step 7: Choose a Hosting Option

To make your website available online, you'll need **web hosting**. You have several options:

1. **Free Hosting (Basic & Limited)**
    - GitHub Pages (Static sites only)
    - Netlify (Easy deployment for static sites)
    - Vercel (Optimized for front-end projects)
2. **Paid Hosting (More Control & Features)**
    - Shared Hosting
    - VPS Hosting
    - Cloud Hosting

Step 8: Get a Domain Name

- Buy a domain.
- Some hosting providers offer a **free domain** for the first year.

Step 9: Upload Your Website Files

Option 1: Using GitHub Pages (Free for Static Sites)

1. Create a GitHub repository.
2. Upload your `index.html`, `styles.css`, `script.js`, and other files.
3. Go to **Settings > Pages** and select the branch to publish.
4. Your site will be available at `https://yourusername.github.io/repository-name/`.

Option 2: Using FTP for Hosting Providers

1. Get FTP credentials from your hosting provider.
2. Use an FTP client like **FileZilla** to upload your files to the `public_html` directory.

Option 3: Deploying with Netlify or Vercel

1. Connect your GitHub repository.
2. Click "Deploy."
3. Netlify/Vercel will generate a public URL.

Step 10: Set Up a Custom Domain (Optional but Recommended)

- If using GitHub Pages, Netlify, or Vercel, follow their instructions to link a custom domain.
- If using paid hosting, update your **DNS settings** to point to your hosting provider's nameservers.

Step 11: Make Your Site Secure with HTTPS

- Most hosting providers **offer free SSL certificates** (e.g., Let's Encrypt).
- If using Netlify/Vercel, HTTPS is automatically enabled.

Step 12: Test on Mobile & Different Browsers

- Test on different internet browsers and mobile devices.

Step 13: Optimize for Speed & SEO

- **Compress images**
- **Minify CSS & JavaScript**
- **Enable caching & CDNs**
- **Add a robots.txt File** (to tell search engines what pages to index and which to ignore).
- **Add a XML sitemap** (to tell search engines about all of pages on your site)

This is a very basic list of SEO tasks, really for just getting start right away but we will explore SEO in more detail in later chapters.

Last Thoughts

Like I said earlier, this is a very basic guide for creating a multi-page website. If you are looking to do E-commerce, or any consulting based website, or data extensive website like a forum, or UGC website, you are definitely better off using a content management system. Let's explore what those are now.

Chapter 7: Content Management Systems

Learning the backend coding components of a website and how they work is just basic foundational information that can be helpful to know, even if you don't decide to build you website from scratch. But chances are if you are a novice then building a website from scratch probably isn't all that practical. Not to mention when it comes to businesses that store a lot of data, you need a website that is easily accessible and is more dynamic. This is where the use of a content management system comes in.

A **Content Management System (CMS)** also sometimes referred to as "website builder" is an all-in-one software application that allows users to create, manage, and modify digital content—typically for websites—without requiring specialized coding knowledge. It provides a user-friendly interface to handle website content, making it easier for individuals and businesses to build and maintain websites efficiently.

Key Features of a CMS:

- **Content Creation & Editing** – Provides a text editor for adding and formatting content.
- **Content Organization** – Allows categorization, tagging, and structuring of content.
- **User Management** – Supports different user roles (e.g., administrators, editors, authors).
- **Templates & Themes** – Enables customization of website appearance without coding.
- **Media Management** – Allows easy uploading and management of images, videos, and files.
- **Plugins & Extensions** – Offers additional functionality through third-party add-ons.

Examples of Popular CMS Platforms:

These are not product endorsements, but below are some examples of common CMS platforms

- **WordPress** – The most widely used CMS, especially for blogs, business sites, and e-commerce.
- **Drupal** – A flexible CMS generally used for complex websites with advanced customization needs.
- **Joomla!** – A middle-ground CMS, that is known for balancing flexibility and ease of use.
- **Shopify** – A CMS designed for e-commerce businesses.
- **Wix** – A drag-and-drop website builder with CMS capabilities.

Choosing the Right CMS

Selecting the right **Content Management System (CMS)** is one of the most important decisions you'll make when building a website. The CMS you choose will determine how easily you can manage content, optimize for search engines, scale your site, and integrate additional tools. With so many options available, it's easy to feel overwhelmed. However, by keeping a few key factors in mind, you can confidently select a CMS that suits your needs.

Here are **ten essential tips** to help you choose the best CMS for your website.

Understand Your Website's Purpose

Before diving into the vast world of CMS platforms, take a step back and consider your website's purpose. Is it a **blog, an online store, a business website, a portfolio, or a community forum**? Different CMS platforms specialize in different areas. For example, **WordPress** is ideal for blogging, while **Shopify** is built for e-commerce. Knowing what you need ensures that you choose a CMS designed for your specific goals.

Look for a User-Friendly Interface

Not everyone is a developer, and a good CMS should be **easy to use** for both technical and non-technical users. A simple, intuitive interface with a **drag-and-drop editor** or a **What You See Is What You Get (WYSIWYG) editor** makes content creation and editing much more manageable. If a CMS requires extensive coding knowledge for basic tasks, it may not be the best fit unless you have a development team.

Ensure Customization & Flexibility

Your website should reflect your **brand identity and business needs**, which means your CMS must support customization. A good CMS offers:

- A variety of **themes and templates** for design flexibility.
- **Plugins or extensions** to add functionality without complex coding.
- Support for **custom code** if you or your developer need more control.

Without these options, you might find yourself stuck with a generic design and limited features.

Prioritize SEO Features

Search engine optimization (SEO) plays a crucial role in attracting visitors to your website. Your CMS should provide **built-in SEO tools** or allow you to install SEO plugins. Essential SEO-friendly features include:

- Customizable **meta titles and descriptions**
- SEO-friendly **URLs and permalinks**
- Image optimization and **alt text support**
- Mobile-friendly themes and **fast-loading pages**

If a CMS lacks strong SEO capabilities, your site may struggle to rank well in search engines. We will explore SEO in more detail in **Chapter 8**.

Consider Scalability & Performance

A website that performs well today should also be able to handle future growth. If you plan to expand your content, increase traffic, or add advanced features, choose a CMS that is **scalable and optimized for performance**. Key factors include:

- A strong **content delivery network (CDN)** for faster page loads.
- Caching features to **reduce server load**.
- The ability to support **high traffic volumes** without crashes.

A CMS that can't handle growth will eventually force you to migrate to a new platform, which can be time-consuming and costly.

Prioritize Security & Regular Updates

Security is **non-negotiable**, especially if you collect user data or process online transactions. A good CMS should have:

- **Frequent updates** to fix security vulnerabilities.
- **SSL support** to encrypt website data.
- **User role management** to control access levels.

Open-source platforms like WordPress rely on community-driven updates, while proprietary CMS platforms like **Wix and Shopify** handle security for you. Choose a CMS that aligns with your **security needs and technical expertise**.

Ensure Mobile Responsiveness

With **mobile traffic surpassing desktop traffic**, your website must be **mobile-friendly**. The CMS you choose should offer **responsive design templates** that automatically adjust to different screen sizes. Google prioritizes mobile-friendly websites in search rankings, so ensuring responsiveness is not just about usability—it's about visibility.

Look for Strong Community Support & Documentation

Even the most user-friendly CMS may present challenges, so having access to **support and resources** is crucial. Before choosing a CMS, check if it offers:

- **Official documentation** for troubleshooting.
- **A strong community forum** where users share solutions.
- **Video tutorials and step-by-step guides**.
- **Customer support (email, chat, or phone)**, if using a paid CMS.

A CMS with an **active support network** ensures that help is available whenever you need it.

Check Integration with Third-Party Tools

Your CMS should integrate with the tools and platforms you rely on, such as:

- **Email marketing services** (Mailchimp, ConvertKit)
- **Analytics tools** (Google Analytics, Hotjar)
- **CRM software** (HubSpot, Salesforce)
- **Social media platforms** for easy sharing
- **Payment gateways** for e-commerce websites

A CMS that lacks integration capabilities may require custom development, increasing costs and complexity.

Consider the Cost & Licensing

Some CMS platforms are **free and open-source** (like WordPress, Joomla), while others operate on **subscription-based pricing** (like Shopify, Wix, and Squarespace). Costs can include:

- **Hosting fees** (for self-hosted CMS like WordPress).
- **Premium themes and plugins** for additional features.
- **Developer costs** if you need custom modifications.

Weigh the **total cost of ownership** against your budget before making a decision.

Final Thoughts: Test Before You Commit

If possible, try a **demo or free trial** before fully committing to a CMS. This allows you to explore its features, interface, and ease of use. Choosing the right CMS is not just about what works today—it's about what will support your website's growth and success in the long run.

By following these ten tips, you'll be well-equipped to make an informed decision and build a website that meets both your present and future needs.

Last Words

I think at this point you should make a decision on which site you wish to have. If you are a beginner or a business owner just get a simple, easy to start with CMS. If you are an intermediate or advanced, then maybe take a crack at building your website from scratch. Also again, make sure you refer back to Chapter 2, to make sure that you choose a proper domain name, and you have a solid URL structure setup. Overall, keep it simple because like I said your real focus should be on getting traffic to your website, and that brings me to Chapter 8.

Section 3: Getting Traffic to Your Website

Chapter 8: SEO Explained

Okay, so hopefully, now you at least have some type of website up, whether you did it by scratch or you used a content management system, it doesn't really matter. Now, you need to focus on how to get traffic to your site, as in actual people who are going to be interested in your content.

Now, there are numerous ways to do this, but typically, website owners focus on two main areas: **SEO (Search Engine Optimization)** and **Content Marketing**. SEO and content marketing go hand in hand, and in fact, when people talk about content marketing, they are definitely talking about SEO.

You see, you can write the best website content, but if people can't find it, as in you have bad SEO, then no one is going to see it. So, I think it is important to first talk about SEO in detail and then segway into the content writing process. Now we already explored SEO a bit in the beginning chapters but that was more from just the "technical" part of SEO, there are other "domains" or parts we also need to explore also. Getting confusing yet? Well, let's get started.

What is SEO

In a nutshell, SEO is all about making your webpages more useful, and easier to read for humans i.e. your website visitors, also it's a bonus that search engines may "reward" you by ranking your website higher.

Additionally, SEO can be thought of as a conceptual framework of thinking process, tactics and strategies that can be used to improve your webpages so that they are better for users and search engines. These activities can be divided up into specific categories or Domains. The following are the most commonly used Domains: Technical SEO, On-Page SEO, and Off-Page SEO. Here is a graphic that you can use to help you make sense of the three domains:

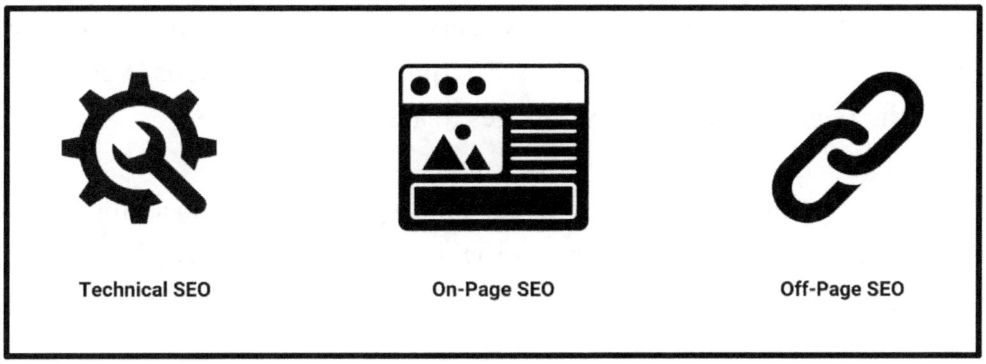

To provide more context to the graphic:

1. **Technical SEO** refers to improving the technical capabilities of a website to make it easier to use and "crawl" or be interpreted by search engines.
2. **On-Page SEO** refers to improving the information and *HTML elements* on a website to make it easier to consume for users, and easier to understand for search engines.
3. **Off-Page SEO**, also sometimes referred to as *Link-building* refers to building "backlinks" or gaining editorial votes to improve a website's notoriety, credibility, and visibility.

Like I said earlier also, content marketing connects deeply with SEO, but it's not a domain persay, in fact the tactics or strategies you use in On-page SEO typically align with content marketing, So just keep that in mind that when you are talking about content you are basically referring to On-page SEO. And again, we already explore Technical SEO a bit earlier when we were talking about robots.txt, XML sitemaps, domains, etc.

We will explore in more detail other technical SEO aspects along with diving into Off-page SEO concepts later. Right now it is good to just have a basic understanding and start connecting some of the dots we covered. Now let's discuss what search engines are in more detail.

Search Engines

There is a lot of competition on the web for the top spots in the search engine results pages. Staying ahead of the competition is imperative, and having an above-average understanding of search engines and how they can help you remain competitive online is vital to SEO success.

Search Engines, are computer programs that allow users to search for information on the Internet. They are essentially a network of computers that use **Spiders**, also known as **Web-Crawlers** or **Bots,** to scour the Internet looking for webpages to add to their **Index.**

Users are then able to access the search engine's index through a user interface; this is usually a page that allows the user to enter **queries** or specific questions into a **search bar** to find webpages that meet their needs.

Here is an example of what a search engine user interface may look like:

Once a query has been entered into the search bar, a search is initiated, and the search engine then displays **Hyperlinks** or access points to the content that addresses the query.

The search engine displays the content in a listed fashion on what is called the **Search Engine Results Pages**, also commonly referred to in the SEO field as the **SERPs**.

Below is an example of what a search engine results page (SERP) may look like:

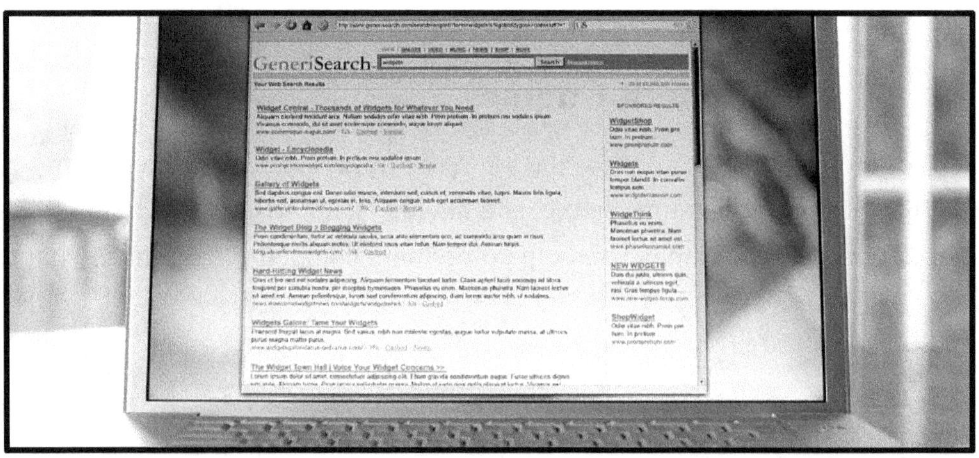

As you can see in the image there is a webpage that includes a “list” of other webpages that a user can visit.

Hopefully now you have a basic idea of what search engines are. Now let’s explore how they work and the three-step process they use to match relevant web content with users' search queries.

How Search Engines Work

In general, all search engines operate on the same three-step process: **Crawling**, **Indexing**, and **Serving Search Results**. Below is a graphic depicting this three-step process:

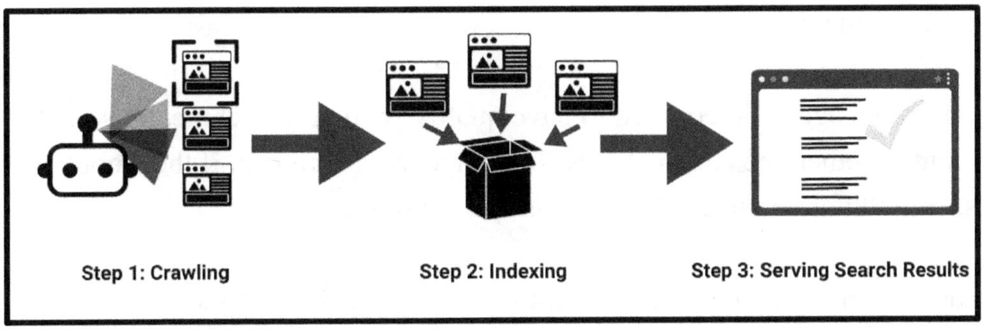

Let’s explore what *Crawling* is and how it works.

Step 1: Crawling

Crawling is a process where the Web Crawler looks for new content (webpages, videos, books, PDF files, images, infographics, articles, research papers, etc.) to add to a search engine’s index.
Web crawlers are able to find this content through a variety of methods such as:

- user-submitted links to the content
- links on previously visited content to the new content (these are called Internal Links)
- or through a file called an XML Sitemap, which is a file that shows search engines where to find each webpage on a website

After the crawler accesses a webpage, if it is considered useful then the *indexation* process begins.

Step 2: Indexation

Indexation occurs once a webpage is rendered, crawled, and analyzed by a search engine. Indexing happens through the following process:

- analyzing a webpage's HyperText Markup Language (HTML) elements
- analyzing a webpage's embedded pictures and videos
- analyzing hyperlinks or citations to another website on the crawled page

After conducting the thorough process, the search engine then determines the viability of the web content for the index based on a variety of factors like:

- the content's writing quality
- the website's technical efficiencies
- the originality of the content

In other words, if a webpage is determined to have quality writing, is technically sound, and possesses original content - then the page is likely to be indexed. Moreover, if the webpage does not pass the "tests," it will not be indexed until revisions are made.

Other factors that influence whether your content will be indexed or not include:

- its relevance to the user's query, its quality
- its ability/inability to be crawled designated by a Noindex Meta Tag, or a *"Disallow Rule"* outlined in the Robots.txt File

Once your webpage or content makes it through the "indexing wringer", it can then be served on the search results pages.

Step 3: Serving Search Results

If a search engine decides to index the content, it will then be served in the search results.

Users can then enter "queries," or words and phrases, to access the indexed content. When a user performs a search, the search engine runs its *algorithm*, or relevancy software, to find web content that it believes best matches what the user is looking for.

The crawler then "ranks" or positions links to the web content on the Search Engine Results Page (SERP). Additionally, the crawler places links to the content it believes most closely matches the users' query at the top of the page. The user can then "click" on one of the links to access the web content.

Essentially, this is how the process works. However, I would visit the documentation of all the major search engines, Google, Bing, Yahoo!, DuckDuckGo, and others, to ensure that you know the specific features and *ranking factors* each search engine uses to determine where to rank your website.

Reviewing each search engine's ranking factors will help you better adjust your tactics, strategies, and content to ensure your website gets the best results.

Last Thoughts about Search Engines

Search engines have become a key component of our everyday lives. As time goes on, they continue improving their algorithms to provide more accurate and relevant user results.

Because of that, it is important for you to stay up to date on the latest algorithm changes to ensure that you are not caught off guard if and when significant changes happen.

Last Words

Hopefully, by now you have a solid understanding of SEO and how it works. Now I want to simplify the SEO doing process by introducing you to my Website Content Writing Process.

Chapter 9: Website Content Writing Process

Every pro is different, but with me, when it comes to writing for my website, my process only consists of four things:

1. **Finding a topic**
2. **Making the content searchable**
3. **Making sure the content is easily accessible**
4. **Sharing it with relevant people**

Here's what I mean; **Step 1. Finding a searchable topic**: This is all about choosing the right *keywords* (important search phrases), relevant topics and themes that your core audience is searching for as the focus of the article. **Step 2. Making the content easy to read and understand**: this is about using *On-Page SEO* to help make the content easier to engage with and also readable for search engines, **Step 3. Making sure the content is easily accessible**: this is about using *Technical SEO* to help make the content easier to access for users and search engines, so this is where speed, performance, security, and overall "accessibility") come in. **Step 4. Sharing it with relevant people**: this last step is all about getting other websites to share and talk about your articles. This process is also referred to as *Link-Building*. '

Let me give you a quick refresher course on each of these SEO concepts, while also introducing some new concepts. It will help you better understand my process.

SEO Concepts Explained

- **Keyword Research:** involves identifying the words and phrases i.e. "*keywords*" that readers use when searching for articles, products, or services similar to what your website offers. So you can include them in your own content to help it become more searchable.

- **On-Page SEO:** generally refers to optimizing the user-facing elements on a webpage that provide basic information about the article, like the title (Title tag), description on what it is about (Meta description), headings etc.

- **Technical SEO**: This domain of SEO focuses on the efficiency and appropriateness of the technical aspects of your website like the structure (think the HTML, CSS, and JavaScript), speed, security, and accessiblity of your website. If you've paid attention to basic website hygiene (domain, URL structure, choosing an appropriate CMS), in addition to, I suppose just being able to setup and operate even the most basic of SEO plugins, you are well on your way to having solid Technical SEO performance.

- **Link-Building:** refers to getting "backlinks" or other websites to share your articles, additionally, it helps search engines see you as a more credible source, and thus they may recommend you more.

As you can see, my process is just basic SEO concepts with all the jargon, tactics, and whimsical ideas left out. I did it like this because I honestly wish someone had done it for me. Wasting your time with silly SEO tactics is a cat-and-mouse game where you never know what the search engines will do next. So what may get you results today, will be obsolete tomorrow. So again, it's better to focus on mastering concepts rather than tactics.

Last Thoughts

So again, when it comes to the website content writing for beginners I recommend you only focus on using the basic SEO concepts like; "Keyword Researching", "On-Page SEO" "Technical SEO" and "Link-Building". But you should avoid tactics, gimmicks, "secret sauce", "mojo", having a poorly running website, too much promotional content, and rushing content production. Also any of that other crap that does not work - just focus on writing content that your readers love, and more specifically you love!

If you focus on that first, higher rankings are a natural side effect. Now that you have an understanding of my website writing process and the SEO concepts that fuel it let's get into the first step, and that is how I go about finding a topic to write about.

Finding Topics To Write About

When it comes to finding a topic to write about it is important that you choose ones that are "searchable" as in there are already articles out there on it, or at least you can find evidence that someone is interested in the topic you are writing about. As in, you can see a lot of people are searching for the topic with specific keywords or search terms.

It's okay to write about new ideas but at least some time should be spent on finding keywords or similar articles that are relevant to your topic idea. Now let's talk about why you should perform keyword research first.

Why Perform Keyword Research

There are a number of reasons to do keyword research first. For one, by performing proper **Keyword research**, beforehand, you can ensure that your articles are able to be found.

Don't be one of those newbs who avoids this step, this is the number 1 reason I see why new bloggers fail at getting more traffic; they don't take the time to research their topic beforehand. So before you start ask yourself these questions:

- What is the main topic of my article?
- What words or phrases do readers use to find similar articles like mine?
- What questions or problems is my article trying to address?
- What keywords do people type into search engines to find my topic?
- What other synonyms, acronyms, slang, or regional variations would people use to find similar articles like mine?

The point of asking yourself these questions is to get a sense of how your audience thinks, talks, and what they would be searching for, again this ensures that you are making content that is relevant and interesting to your audience, and also so you make the best use of your researching time. Now here's how to research:

So again think of keyword research not only as a way to find topics to blog about but also as a way to help you better gauge your own expertise, and whether or not you can ACTUALLY create the content.

Again guys the goal is to save money and time, but also to establish "Topical Authority" which is when readers and search engines start to see you as a credible source on a topic. Okay now that you started your keyword research let's go over how to pick the best ones.

How To Do Keyword Research

You might hear other SEO professionals talk about all these tools you can use and all these metrics you should follow like "search volume", "search intent" and "competition score", but it's really all about *relevancy*, as in choosing topics/keywords that people are actually searching for, and talking about.

Don't over-stress it. Using tools can be helpful but it's so easy to get caught up in choosing the "perfect keyword" that has the highest volume, or the lowest competition that you end up avoiding talking about critical topics that your unique readers want to hear your perspective on.

So again start with the basics. Once I have a topic in mind, I then do some minor keyword research just to make sure when I am writing I do not miss anything. The first thing I use is the *Auto-Suggest* feature of search engines.

Auto-Suggest

When just starting I recommend just using the *Auto-Suggest* feature of your preferred search engine. The auto-suggest feature is a tool on platforms like Google that shows users recommended keywords that may be related to what they are looking for. Let me give you an example. I typed in the keyword ***bread recipe,*** as you can see in the screenshot below, Google recommended some different search terms:

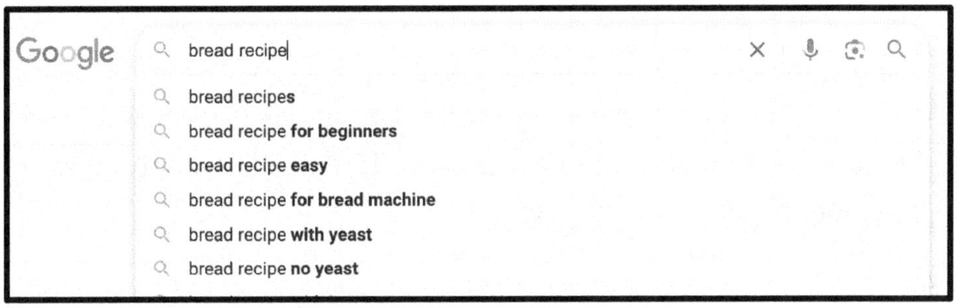

- *Bread recipes for beginners*
- *Bread recipe easy*
- *Bread recipe for bread machine*
- *Bread recipe with yeast*
- *Bread recipe no yeast*

Now these are all in theory their own unique recipes, but by using this auto-suggest feature you might see if there are some keywords that are also relevant to your content.

If my bread recipe also uses *active dry yeast*, *a bread machine*, and it's for *beginners* I should work these related terms into my recipe page somewhere. The point of doing this is to make your webpage more "relevant" and more "searchable".

Refer to Competitors

Another way to find relevant keywords is when in doubt just look at other bloggers who have similar articles; What I would do is make a list of similar articles to mine and then look to see what keywords they use. Check out this screenshot below from a blogger who made a bread recipe post:

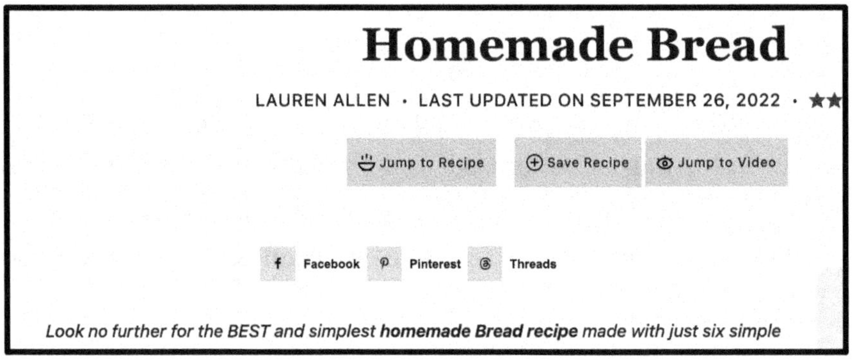

As you can see in the screenshot they mentioned, "homemade bread recipe". Mentioning "homemade" may be a good idea to use in my post if I was doing it. Hopefully, you can tell that by taking the time to research your competitors, you will be able to identify gaps in your own article and opportunities for new keywords to target.

Look At Forums and Message Boards

Forums and message boards are another great place to find blog ideas that maybe haven't been touched on yet. So they can be a good place to find article ideas. Also, they are a good place to find other relevant search terms that you might want to include in your writing. Check out the screenshot below from a forum poster, they want to know a sandwich loaf recipe.

That could easily be another new recipe to create, or I can take this keyword and apply it to my article if it is relevant. So again I would do the same thing, just look through the different forums, make a list of different topics, and choose the one that you feel is the best for you to write about or is the most applicable to your article.

Keyword Research Tools

Keyword research tools are usually my last afterthought because it's so easy to get caught up in all the graphs, and green lights, that you end up getting obsessive with a keyword. But they can be helpful if you need help with just finding more related search terms, but again I wouldn't lean on these tools for everything.

What To Do With Your Keywords

So with your keywords, I would write them down and keep them in a spreadsheet so you can easily refer to them as you write your content. You can see an example below in the screenshot. The spreadsheet doesn't have to be fancy, just functional.

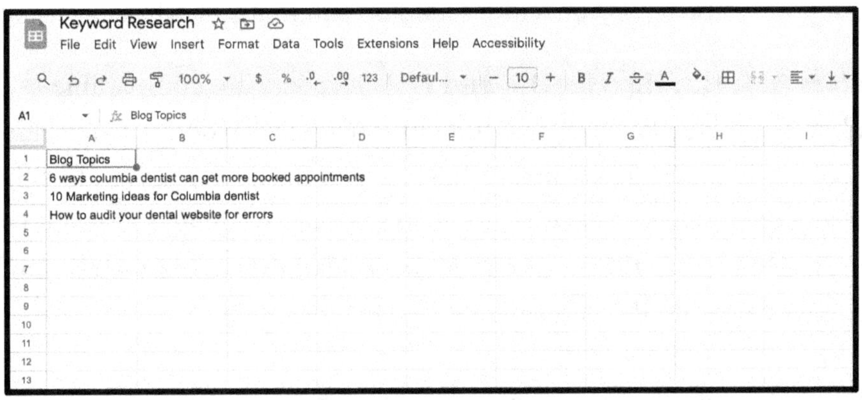

Last Thoughts

To close out this section, Keyword research should be more about finding relevant topics that people are already reading, rather than chasing the most viral topic you can find. Also, it's about finding other related terms that can help you better improve the searchability and semantics of your writing.

Again, keyword tools can be helpful but you should use them as a supplement, not as an end-all be-all. Okay so once you have a topic in mind, and some keywords it's time to start writing, let's go over how I would structure my SEO content.

Structuring SEO Content

Hopefully, by now you have a solid blog topic idea with some related keywords that you want to write about. For the next step, you need to start actually writing your article, like I said earlier, when it comes to writing SEO content and making it easier to read and understand for search engines you need to adhere to **On-Page SEO** "elements" like; **Title tags**, **Meta Descriptions**, and **Headings**. Here's some more additional detail on what they are:

- **Title Tag**: These tags function similarly to the title of a book or movie, as the tag provides a quick insight into the content and relevance of the webpage to a user's query. The title text is essential in enticing users to click on a result and providing them with valuable information.
- **Meta Description**: The Meta Description is the second piece of text a user encounters in each search result. Much like the title tag, its purpose is to captivate and persuade readers to visit your webpage by providing a quick summary of what the webpage is about.
- **Headers (H1, H2, H3, H4, H5, and H6)**: Headers are comparable to chapters found in a novel or book. Headers are used to help separate and identify ideas and paragraphs in web content. The usage of headers allows you to show your readers that they are going into more detail about a specific topic. Also, headers play a relevant role in search engines, as they assist them in better understanding the organization of your text on the page and evaluating its convenience for any searcher.

Additionally, you want to pay attention to web writing mechanics like the structure, formatting, and readability of your content like:

- **Keyword placement**: Making sure you use your keywords in your Title tag, Meta description, and throughout your article. Additionally, you can include keywords in your URL, to help with readability as well.
- **Paragraph Length**: Keeping paragraphs short and readable for a better user experience.
- **Bullet Points and Lists**: Breaking information into digestible formats to enhance readability.
- **Internal Links**: Linking to other relevant pages within the website to provide more context and improve SEO.

- **External Links**: Linking to other relevant websites/webpages on other sites that provide additional information or context.
- **Images:** Adding images can help with improving comprehension, additionally you can add *Image Alt Text* to help readers who are visually impaired and use screen reader software.

I hope that you were able to pick up from reading the suggestions, that the overall point of On-Page SEO is to make your writing more appropriate for a web format. Not so much to be picky about what you write or your unique writing style. These are not tactics, but instead just basic web etiquette.

Just imagine how hard it would be to read online if there weren't any titles, headings, or links, or if the writer didn't break up ideas with bullet points or short paragraphs. It would be frustrating as hell! So again, taking the time just to structure your article is critical to SEO success. Now let's discuss how to put these mechanics in practice.

How To Structure A Webpage

So when it comes to structuring your articles it's important to just focus on the basics. Let me give you an example to help you wrap your head around this. Below I included an example of an SEO piece of Content that I wrote for a made-up client's blog post:

Sample Page Copy

Keywords: Business credit, Business credit card guide, How to build business credit
URL: www.samsbanking.com/blog/**how-to-build-business-credit**.com

Title Tag
<title> **How to build business credit** in 5 steps | Sam's Banking </title>

Meta Description
<meta name="description" content=" **Building business credit** can help an entrepreneur grow their business, by building a credit history, and improving access to capital, here's how to do it." /
>

Headings
<h1> **How to build business credit** in 5 steps </h1>
<h2> What is **business credit?**</h2>
<h2> **1. Register your business** </h2>
<h2> **2. Register for a Dun & Bradstreet number** </h2>
<h2> **3. Apply for a business credit card** </h2>

<h2> **4. Register for relevant net 30 accounts** </h2>
<h2> **5. Pay all bills on time and avoid tax liens** </h2>
<h2> **How to maintain your credit** <h2>

So as you can see from the example, I first wrote the *keywords/topics* that my article is addressing - I do this to help with writing the actual article, which I'll show you in a second. Also, I structure out the URL, or the unique web address that my article is at, you see I again put the keyword in there too, again this helps with remembering the address for readers.

Next, I wrote a Title Tag, a Meta description, and I created Headings, for this example, there were only H1, and H2 headings used but, again H3 - H6 is available as well.

Lastly, once I have the basic On-Page SEO mechanics done, I then start writing my article, this is where the "web writing mechanics" come into play I mentioned like using bullet points and shorter paragraphs. This example is going to get quite long, so I am just going to show you with the first two paragraphs:

<h1> **How to build business credit** in 5 steps </h1>
Starting or growing a business often requires access to capital, and building strong business credit is a key step to making that happen. Business credit allows you to separate your personal finances from your business which makes it:

- Easier to secure loans
- Lower interest rates,
- Gain favorable payment terms with vendors.

Here's a beginner-friendly guide to help you **how to build business credit** in just five steps!

<h2> What is **business credit?**</h2>

Business credit is a track record of a business's financial responsibility, similar to personal credit for individuals. Lenders, suppliers, and financial institutions use your business credit to evaluate your company's ability to pay back loans and meet financial obligations.

A strong business credit score can open doors to various financing opportunities and better terms. It's vital because it allows you to obtain credit in the name of your business, without involving your personal credit, which minimizes personal financial risk.

Again looking at the example I showed, as you can see web writing mechanics were used. For the *keyword placement,* I bolded it to show what keywords were used, again paragraphs were deliberately kept short to help with skimming, and bullet points were added to help with digesting the information better.

Additionally to the example, we can add *Images*, *Internal* and *External links*. With images, it's important to remember that they should be "semantic" and not just decorative so for instance with the article:

<table>
<tr><th>Image 1</th><th>Image 2</th></tr>
<tr><td>

This is a better image:

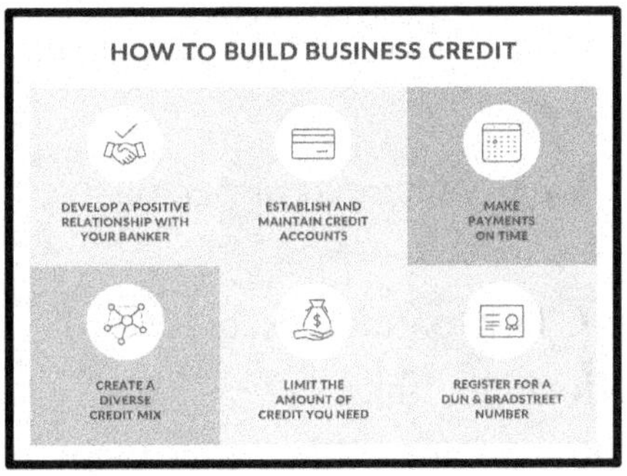

Cited from: https://www.johnsonfinancialgroup.com/resources/blogs/business-guidance/how-to-build-business-credit/

</td><td>

Then this image:

</td></tr>
</table>

The reason is Image 1, is more semantic it shows the steps that are being addressed in the article which again can help people who are skimming. While Image 2 is just decorative it doesn't necessarily communicate what the article is about - does this make sense?

For links, some good pages we could link to could be another related article on the same website about repairing business credit, so let's say the reader already has credit but it's in bad standing and they need help.

Another good link(s) could be links to some different banks that offer business credit. The "anchor text" or the clickable blue text that will be highlighted to show these links is below:

Hyperlinks

Add a hyperlink with anchor text "how to repair business credit" —-> https://www.samsbanking.com/how-repair-business-credit

Add a hyperlink with anchor text "banks that offer business credit" —-> https://www.banking.com/banks-offering-business-credit

As you can see I made the anchor text semantic as well, I included keywords to help with readability, this is another great tip - search engines dig this too!

Last Thoughts

That's the overall basics to writing a web article that is SEO-friendly and easy to read and comprehend for your audience. Now I am not going to go too much into detail on the overall mechanics of how I actually figure out what to write in the tags, and the content itself, as this is considered to be "copywriting" and that's for another book. But I will give you some just quick tips:

1. **Use of Power Words in Your Headlines**: Including emotionally charged or persuasive words that trigger interest and action.
2. **Add Call-To-Actions**: Writing direct and action-oriented CTAs to guide users toward desired actions (e.g., signing up, making a purchase, or clicking a link).
3. **Storytelling**: Engaging readers by telling a story or painting a picture that draws them in emotionally.
4. **Urgency and Scarcity**: Creating a sense of urgency (e.g., limited-time offers) to prompt action.
5. **Social Proof**: Using testimonials, case studies, or statistics to build credibility and persuade the audience.

All of these are not required, because they are more for marketing a product or a service, but they can be helpful tips for bloggers to help with promoting their own offers. =

Making Sure The Content Is Easily Accessible

This part of my process is all about "auditing" or reviewing the technical components of your website to make sure that it is running at optimal performance. I am going to share with you some basic **Technical SEO** tasks that are pretty easy to follow and implement. These tasks focused on identifying issues with SEO components like:

- **Core Web Vitals metrics**: This is where making your website fast is important. Also updating web hosting or your content management system can be a great way to start improving your site speed, performance and structure. In other words the "*core web vitals metrics*".
- **Accesibility: URLs**, this is basic SEO; making your URLs are easy to read and understand is just basic common SEO sense, but also making sure your URLs are

accessible. This where making sure "links" are not broken (as in attending to **Server response codes** like **404s)** but also it overlaps with *indexing*.

- **Indexing:** This is where the **Robots.txt File** comes in, if you setup a basic SEO plugin on your CMS this is taken care of. Also the **XML Sitemap File.** Same thing, if you got a basic CMS with an SEO plugin this is good to go. I am still mentioning the Robots.txt and XML sitemap because again it is just basic hygiene. We'll also dig into more intricate things like *HTTPs* and *SSL Certificates*.
- **Enhancements:** This is about *Schema Markup*, again sounds intricate but it is really quite simple it's all about making your content more "readable" and "understandable" to search engines.

Now let me share with you a quick step by step clean-up guide that encompasses these more exquisite SEO concepts that I just mentioned. This is interpolated from my book: The Technical SEO handbook. I did mention a few specific tools from the search engine: Google that you may need to use to accomplish these tasks but they are all free. Again not a plug - these are just generally the standard tools that you can use to accomplish these tasks.

Step 1: Check For Multiple Versions of Your Website

Having multiple versions of your website is normal. However, you want to make sure each "version" goes to the same site. For example, `https://www.bouncerank.com` and `http://www.bouncerank.com` are two different versions of my old site bouncerank but they should all go to the same site.

How to check the multiple versions of your site:

1. Go to your preferred web browser
2. Type in these 4 different versions of the homepage URL:
    - `http://example.com`
    - `https://example.com`
    - `http://www.example.com`
    - `https://www.example.com`

They should all redirect to one URL. If not, set up *301 redirects* to avoid duplicate content problems.

Step 2: Check Indexing

Review the indexed pages of your website in search engines like Google. Compare the number of indexed pages to the actual number of pages on your site to ensure there are no discrepancies.

Here's how to see if you are having indexing issues:

1. Log into your Google Search Console account.
2. Select the "Index coverage" report in Google Search Console and review the result.

You can also follow up by running a crawl on a website crawling software, this will provide you with additional insights on specific pages and issues to fix.

Step 3: Evaluate Website Speed

Check your website's loading speed using tools like Google PageSpeed Insights. This tools will provide insights on areas to optimize, such as image compression, caching, minifying CSS and JavaScript, and reducing server response time.

To check your website's loading speed, do the following:

1. Go to your preferred browser and visit https://pagespeed.web.dev.
2. On the page speed insights website, enter your homepage URL and other important web pages on your site.
3. View the results and see where you need to make improvements.

You want to make a habit of checking your website speed regularly, especially if you website is very picture-heavy, images naturally take up a lot of space and can slow down your website. So keep that in mind as you are optimizing your website for speed.

Step 4: Assess Mobile-Friendliness

Ensure your website is mobile-friendly by using Google's Mobile-Friendly Test or similar tools. Mobile responsiveness is crucial, as search engines prioritize mobile-friendly websites in their rankings. Optimize your website's design and layout to ensure a seamless experience across different devices.

To check your website's mobile friendliness do the following:

1. Using your preferred web browser visit: https://search.google.com/test/mobile-friendly.
2. Enter your website into the test bar.
3. Wait for your results (it may take a minute or two).
4. Review the results (take a screenshot so you can refer back to it later and measure your website's progress over time).

Since 2015, having a mobile-friendly website has been a key factor that search engines use to rank websites. So it is worth your time to invest in a website that is mobile-friendly.

Step 5: Review URL Structure

URLs that are descriptive, have relevant keywords in them, are short and readable, and are preferred by search engines. Also, they are much easier to remember and read for humans.

Here's how to review yours:

1. Gather a list of all your website's URLs.
2. Examine them, Are they descriptive and user-friendly? Do they contain relevant keywords?
3. Make note of this, and for new URLs make sure they are easy to read.

We recommend to clients to not change URLs unless it makes sense to do so. As in the page is not performing well. The reason is, that you will run into major indexing issues. So generally speaking, keep your URLs the same.

Step 6: Check the Robots.txt File

A Robots.txt file is a text file that contains directives for web crawlers (such as Google) that tell them which pages they can and cannot crawl and index. As I mentioned earlier, it is typically found at `/robots.txt`

Here's how to check your robots.txt:

1. Go to the browser and type your domain name in the address bar. At the end of your domain name, include this slug: `/robots.txt`.
2. Type enter, and then view your robots.txt file to ensure it aligns with your website's requirements and goals.
3. Look for User-Agent directives, Review the Allow and Disallow directives to ensure they accurately reflect the areas of your website that should be allowed or disallowed for

crawling. If you have specified the location of your XML sitemap in your robots.txt file, ensure that the sitemap URL is accurate.

4. Validate the Robots.txt File, you can use online tools or validators specifically designed for this purpose. Sign in to the webmaster tools provided by search engines like Google, Bing, or Yandex. Locate the section where you can test or fetch your robots.txt file. Use this feature to ensure that search engines can access and interpret your robots.txt file correctly.

Regularly monitor your website's behavior and search engine crawling patterns to ensure your robots.txt file is functioning as intended. Make updates to the file when necessary, such as when you want to allow or disallow access to specific pages or directories.

Step 7: Check XML Sitemap

An XML sitemap is a file that lists all the URLs on your website and how to find them.

Your XML sitemap is typically located in the root directory of your website. It is often named "`sitemap.xml`" or similar. If you're not sure where to find it, you can check your website's robots.txt file, which usually contains a reference to the sitemap's location.

To check your XML sitemap, follow these steps:

1. Go to the browser and type your domain name in the address bar. At the end of your domain name, including this slug: `/sitemap.xml`
2. Type enter, and then view your sitemap file, Check the structure of your XML sitemap to ensure it follows the proper format. The sitemap should be well-formed XML and include necessary elements like `<urlset>`, `<url>`, `<loc>`, and `<lastmod>`. Each URL entry should have its corresponding `<loc>` element, indicating the URL of the page.
3. Review the list of URLs in your XML sitemap. Make sure that all important pages of your website are included. Check for any missing or omitted pages that should be present in the sitemap. If any URLs are missing, you may need to update your sitemap generation process.
4. Check that your XML sitemap is error-free, you can use online XML sitemap validators. Several free tools are available that allow you to submit your XML sitemap for validation.
5. Once you have confirmed that your XML sitemap is accurate and error-free, submit it to search engines.

6. Sign in to the webmaster tools provided by search engines like Google, Bing, or Yandex, and locate the section where you can submit or add your sitemap. Follow the instructions provided by the specific search engine to submit your XML sitemap.

Regularly monitor your XML sitemap to ensure it stays up to date. Whenever you add or remove pages from your website, make sure to update your XML sitemap accordingly. Additionally, periodically check your search engine's webmaster tools for any reported issues or errors related to your XML sitemap.

Step 8: Verify HTTPS and SSL Certificates

Check if your website is secured with HTTPS and has a valid SSL certificate. HTTPS is an important ranking factor, and it ensures secure communication between your website and users. Make sure all internal and external links are using the HTTPS protocol.

Here's how to do it:

1. Type your website in your browser's address bar, and press enter.
2. Check to see if a "green lock" is displayed on the left side of your browser.
3. Spot-check a few other pages on your website to see if the lock is displayed.
4. If it is not, you need to contact your hosting provider to get an SSL certificate installed.

Having a secure website is not just about ranking, it is also important to have if you plan on keeping sensitive or personal information about your users on your website.

Step 9: Audit for Duplicate and Low-Value Content

Google has a limited amount of time that it spends on each website to find content. This "crawl budget" or the amount of time they will spend before moving on, can be affected by having pages that are duplicates, or just don't have value (Like archive pages, category pages, UTM parameters, tag pages, etc.). All of these types of pages should be removed from your website.

Here is how you find these types of pages:

1. Go to your preferred browser and go to Google.com.
2. Check how many pages are in Google's index by typing `site:example.com` into the Google search bar.

3. Additionally, in Google search console, check your "Indexing Coverage" report to see if there are any pages that were "crawled but not indexed" or that are labeled as "duplicates" in the report.

These "Zombie", or dead pages are best to delete or no index, doing so can improve your crawl rate and rankings.

Step 10: Check for Broken Links

A broken link is a link on your website that does not work. Broken links are basically dead ends. Have you ever gone on a website, clicked a link, and got a "404" error? Broken links are frustrating and it's important to know if you have any.

You can check for broken links by:

1. Log into your Google Search Console account.
2. Go to your "Index Coverage" report view your website's URL and identify the ones that have a 404 error.
3. Take note of the broken links and create 301 redirects.

Having too many broken links is not just troublesome for search engines, it is also a major user experience issue. This is why we often recommend to clients that when attending to technical SEO, this is one of the first things they should go about fixing.

Step 11: Check For Enhancements

When Google shows your content in the search results there may be times when they choose to show it larger, or more prominent these "rich results" can be influenced by you with structured data, or Schema markup.

To check to see if your website has structured data do this:

1. Go to Google Search console.
2. Go to the "enhancements menu", and under this menu, you can see all the structured data that is currently on your website. If there is none, then you don't have any structured data.
3. Use a schema markup generator to generate the code for the markup. For blogs use article schema, for product pages use product schema, for local businesses use local business schema. Refer to this post for more markup types to add.
4. Implement one instance of schema in the <head> HTML section of each page.

Schema markup is not only great for getting a rich snippet, but also for helping Google understand the content of your website and making your website more accessible to users.

Last Words

Like I said these are some steps that can help you improve your technical SEO, which essentially will help you improve your overall website traffic. Follow all the steps, they are will help you improve your website traffic. Also, don't be worried if there is a step that just doesn't fit you or you find after doing the step it just doesn't make a difference. That's okay, unfortunately when it comes to technical SEO, normally the best way to improve your overall website performance is to upgrade your web hosting, and/or your content management system. Now let's get on to the next step.

Sharing Your Content

Okay, so once you have a solid article written, and your website is at a reasonable performance level, it is now time to get the article out there, and promote it. When it comes to content creation this is yet another major mistake newbs make - they just think search engines are going to magically send traffic to the article.

Not a chance my friend! You have to start building up some credibility for the article. You can do this one way by getting what is called "backlinks", also known as editorial votes, and the process of getting these backlinks is called Link-building. Let me expand, backlinks essentially are instances where another website links or shares your article, and the reason this matters to search engines is because it makes the website owner seem more credible.

I think this is obvious though, obviously, you would be more swayed to read an article from someone who has been quoted and shared thousands of times versus someone who is new. But that's still not to say a beginner can't get traction. You just have to have a strategy and be patient.

How To Get Backlinks

So when it comes to getting your content out there and actually having someone share it, it really comes down to making sure you follow steps 1, 2, and 3 of my process, and then finally start finding different website owners to share your content with. It's not rocket science. The main ways I use are:

- **Sending an email to relevant blog owners:** There's nothing wrong with sending a "cold email" to different blog owners in your niche and just seeing if they would share your article. Now I would actually take the time to get to know them first, or even offer payment but the key thing to remember is just be a regular human being, if your article is good, and you reach out to enough people there definitely will be one person who will link back to you. It's a start but not an end-all-be-all.
- **Using social media:** Another great way to get the word out about your blog posts is to create different social media accounts and share your posts on them. Now of course you need to make sure you are actually engaging with other people to build up a following, but once you do you may find that people will start to interact with you and share your content. Additionally, just ask people to do it, the worst they can say is no, or just not respond.
- **Guest blogging:** Reaching out to blog owners and asking to collaborate or do a guest post is a great way to get the word out about you as a blogger in general. Additionally, it can help with getting your post found, in your guest post you can link up your previous post so that more people can see them.
- **Paid outreach:** Over time the idea of paying for backlinks has become less taboo; the truth is professionals have been doing this forever, but they just weren't being vocal about it. Honestly, I think this is why link-building has had such an unnatural feel to it. People think it is so confusing to do. When honestly it is really just as simple as offering payment for a link.

  The truth is everyone loves money, so I am not going to be facetious and tell you that this method is not being actively employed. But I will say that search engines like Google don't like paid placements, and in fact, they mention in their documentation that you should not be paying for links with the intent to manipulate rankings. Also, if you pay for a link placement it should be designated with the HTML attribute "sponsored". Again, I am not recommending this method to you, but this is what people do.

Avoid Rushing The Process

Now again, I know what you are thinking - "Is that all I can do?". Unfortunately yes, there isn't a secret method to just getting a bunch of backlinks overnight - well there are methods, but they will do WAY more harm than good.

This is why I recommend to new bloggers that patience is key. If you feel like your articles are great, don't wait for search engines or people to find you, hit the ground running and share your content around, and even pay if you are that in need.

But whatever you shouldn't do, do not try to rush things by buying any of those backlink packages you see on freelancer sites. Buying backlinks in bulk are considered to be spam by search engines, so this can get your website removed from results. So again, buyer beware! If you are going to pay, make sure you properly vet each website you are buying from, and do it one at a time.

Last Thoughts

I know that a lot of people who read this book may have been expecting me to go into ravishing details about all the ways to build links, but honestly, I don't think they matter.

I think what's more important is having amazing content, and then taking the time to let other website owners know about it. But, I am certainly not one of those professionals that says; *"just make good content, and people will find it on their own"*.

The key thing to take away from this step is that; you have to be able to persuade a website owner to want to link back to you. This doesn't happen overnight. You have to build relationships with these website owners naturally.

My best advice is to start with creating content that is of value, and then reach out to website owners to give it an extra boost. In other words, there is not a conveyor belt-like method to getting backlinks, it takes time and consistency. Okay, there you have it, that is my 4 step process for making website content, let's get into the last chapter.

Last Words

As you can see, the website writing process can be very simple if you make it so. For a beginning website owner, I think this is more than enough information to help you get started with creating content that is enjoyable but also searchable.

With creating website content it is very important to take care of all of the important mechanics and attention to detail beforehand. So the longer it takes to implement sound suggestions, that are rooted in conceptualization and not tactics, the longer it may take to see results that you want.

Writing content for websites has become too much about chasing virality, that there are so many pseudo-experts running around on the internet, trying to get as many people to read their content as possible by writing about what they think sounds good, and not necessarily rooted in any real knowledge or research.

The truth is too many website owners, and even digital marketing agencies do this, they make the mistake of trying to mimic or pretend that they know a subject just so they can create content for it.

This is why it is so important to know your lane. If you do not know a topic it is worth the time and money to consult with someone who is in that field and knows the vernacular and the nuances of their industry.

This will help you make better content that is not only more credible but something readers can respect more. Also only make content that readers will find value in, not just content that you think might get the highest ranking.

For instance, if you are a food blogger don't spend your time trying to chase every viral recipe, instead focus on creating content for recipes that you know how to make FIRST, and then later down the road as you get feedback on your content you will discover other content ideas that are worth exploring.

Here's another example, if you are a journalist focusing on writing articles on current events is always a good place to start, but do your research first to see if it's a topic that you can actually speak on. When creating content you should never want to share misinformation, again this is why it is so important to consult industry experts for content creation.

The fact of the matter is that you should take your time with content creation, and be sure that you are always creating website pages that will be useful for your readers and search engines as well.

Section 4: Last Thoughts

Chapter 10: Conclusion

Hopefully by reaching the end of the book, you now have the tools, and strategies to succeed in creating a website that is not only a good user experience, but also is able to be found and rank well in the search engines. The key thing to remember about creating a website is that you need to keep it simple.

Like I said, in the introduction of the book you are going to be bombarded with so much information, and so many product endorsements on the newest platforms or tools to use. Don't fall for this, the goal of your website is to impress your audience and get them to convert and do what you want them to do on their.

If you make the mistake of convoluting things, you are going to run into the same trap that many of the big companies that have millions of dollars to spend on website developments have fallen into. You are going to overdue it and your website will fail to deliver the result you were looking for. Here is a list of tips I have for running a successful website long-term

1. Prioritize User Experience (UX)

- Make navigation simple and intuitive.
- Optimize page load speed (use caching, optimize images, and minimize scripts).
- Ensure mobile-friendliness; over half of web traffic comes from mobile devices.
- Use a clean and readable design (proper fonts, spacing, and contrast).

2. SEO Best Practices

- Conduct keyword research to target relevant search terms.
- Optimize on-page SEO (meta tags, headings, internal linking).
- Focus on high-quality, long-form content that provides value.
- Regularly update content to keep it fresh and relevant.
- Use structured data markup to enhance search engine visibility.

3. Content Strategy & Blogging Tips

- Create a content calendar to maintain consistency.
- Focus on evergreen content that stays relevant over time.

- Mix up content formats (blogs, videos, infographics, podcasts).
- Encourage user-generated content, like reviews and testimonials.
- Answer common customer questions through blog posts and FAQs.

4. Strong Call-to-Actions (CTAs)

- Use clear and compelling CTAs to guide visitors toward conversions.
- Experiment with CTA placements (above the fold, within content, at the end of articles).
- A/B test different CTA designs and wording for better performance.

5. Email Marketing & Lead Generation

- Offer lead magnets (free e-books, checklists, templates) to grow your email list.
- Use pop-ups and embedded forms without being intrusive.
- Segment email lists for personalized communication.
- Automate email campaigns to nurture leads and convert them.

6. Monetization & Revenue Growth

- Explore multiple revenue streams: ads, affiliate marketing, digital products, memberships.
- Offer premium or gated content for exclusive access.
- Optimize product pages for better e-commerce conversions.
- Use upselling and cross-selling techniques effectively.

7. Social Media & Community Building

- Promote website content on social media platforms.
- Engage with followers and encourage discussions.
- Join relevant online communities and forums to drive targeted traffic.
- Collaborate with influencers and industry leaders for exposure.

8. Performance Tracking & Analytics

- Use analytics to monitor traffic sources, user behavior, and conversions.
- Track bounce rates and identify problem areas for improvement.
- Set up goal tracking in your analytics software to measure success.
- Adjust strategies based on performance insights.

9. Website Security & Maintenance

- Use SSL certificates to encrypt data and protect user privacy.
- Keep plugins, themes, and CMS software updated.
- Regularly back up your website to prevent data loss.
- Monitor for broken links and fix them to improve SEO and user experience.

10. Adaptability & Continuous Learning

- Stay updated on industry trends and algorithm changes.
- Experiment with new content formats, tools, and strategies.
- Engage with audience feedback and refine your approach.
- Be flexible and willing to pivot when necessary.

Last Words

Again, I hope these tips help you out! Again just remember to keep things simple, and just focus on making sure your users love your website. If you just focus on that, then you can never go wrong. Good luck on your website journey!

About the Author

Roggie (Raj) Clark, is an 9-year SEO professional and owner of the SEO agency; *Bounce Rank.* Prior to joining the SEO industry, Raj was a web developer and school teacher. It was through creating his own websites, and wanting a career change from teaching, that Raj stumbled across the world of SEO.

Since joining the field nearly a decade ago, Raj has worked on a wide range of campaigns, from eCommerce, to B2B, Healthcare, enterprise companies and marketing agencies in the United States.

He is regarded as an expert, and guru by his colleagues, and the SEO industry. Raj currently lives in Maryland with his sister and niece

.

Consulting or Coaching Services

I know that from reading this book, it simply may not be enough information for you or you may require more personalized support with your unique business situation.

So because of that, I'm offering the opportunity to receive consulting or coaching from me on SEO. I can offer support with:

- Creating SOPs (Standard Operating Procedures)
- Creating SEO strategies
- SEO implementation
- Content suggestions
- Technical audits
- Web design/migrations
- Competitor analysis
- Keyword research
- SEO career coaching

If you are interested in any of these services, or would like to request more information, for a specific need you may have.

Please email me at **bounceranksseo@gmail.com**. In your email, please include the following information:

- Your name
- The business you represent (if applicable)
- Team size (if applicable)
- The type of service you would like to receive
- The length of service needed
- Any other important information I should know

My administrative assistant will email you back within 24 - 48 hours with rates, and an information sheet for you to review. Thank you so much for your time and interest.

www.ingramcontent.com/pod-product-compliance
Lightning Source LLC
LaVergne TN
LVHW082353200926
848481LV00012B/3552
* 9 7 9 8 3 4 8 3 1 6 6 6 2 *